DAVID MILNE

David Milne June 1936

David Milne

EDITED BY IAN M. THOM

with essays by Megan Bice, Christine Boyanoski, Lora Senechal Carney, François-Marc Gagnon, David P. Silcox & Ian M. Thom

The Vancouver Art Gallery
and
McMichael Canadian Art Collection
in association with
Douglas & McIntyre

Douglas & McIntyre Ltd.
1615 Venables Street
Vancouver, British Columbia
V5L 2H1

Printed and bound in Canada

Canadian Cataloguing in Publication Data:

Main entry under title:
David Milne
        Includes bibliographical references.
        ISBN 088894-740-2
 1   Milne, David, 1882–1953
 I   Thom, Ian M. (Ian MacEwan), 1952–
 II Vancouver Art Gallery
 III McMichael Canadian Art Collection
ND249.M54D38 1991   759.11   C91-091344-7

The publisher gratefully acknowledges the assistance of the Visual
Arts Section of the Canada Council in the publication of this book.
Like the exhibition from which it springs, the book has benefitted
from the sponsorship of Trimark Investment Management Inc. Sponsorship coordination: Arts and Communications Counselors.

Frontispiece:

1 SUMMER COLORS. Six Mile Lake, June 1936.
Oil on canvas, 31.1 x 36.2. Milne Family Collection.

*White, Black, Blue and Green. Day after day in
summer, on any Canadian lake, the man in the canoe
sees these colors, these simple shapes and these wide
blank spaces.*
– David Milne, catalogue for
Exhibition of Little Pictures,
Mellors Galleries, 24 Oct–7 Nov 1936

The thing that 'makes' a picture is the thing that 'makes' dynamite – compression. – David Milne

■ An exhibition also creates a picture. The gathering of many paintings, prints and watercolours which are normally spread far apart provides a form of compression which, if successful, allows us to form a powerful impression of an artist's career and work. The McMichael Canadian Art Collection and the Vancouver Art Gallery are delighted to join with our sister institution, the National Gallery of Canada, in presenting a major exhibition of the work of David Milne, out of which this book has grown.

The project has been realized by many staff at both institutions, but particular thanks must go to Ian Thom, Senior Curator, Vancouver Art Gallery and Megan Bice, Curator, McMichael Canadian Art Collection. The complex task of assembling the works and coordinating photography was ably carried out by Sandra Cooke and Heather Ardies at the McMichael Canadian Art Collection.

Trimark Investment Management Inc. has generously supported this project from its inception, and we very much appreciate the spirit of encouragement shown by Arthur Labatt, President, and Richard Hamm, Senior Vice President, in helping us bring Milne's work the attention it deserves.

In addition, Amex Bank of Canada and the *Financial Post* have assisted in bringing this exhibition to reality. The project would not have been possible without generous grants from the Department of Communications.

The exhibition has benefitted greatly from the assistance, support and research of David Milne, Jr. We are grateful to the Milne family for their support of the project as a whole.

Milne throughout his life maintained an absolute devotion to his art. This book and this exhibition – the largest show of Milne's work since the 1950s – will expose a new generation of Canadians to his genius and reveal the strength, power and beauty of his life's work.

Barbara Ann Tyler, Director,
McMichael Canadian Art Collection

Willard Holmes, Director,
Vancouver Art Gallery

Directors' Foreword

2 PAINTING PLACE III. A Big Moose subject, painted at Weston, Ontario, 1930. Oil on canvas, 51.5 x 66.4. National Gallery of Canada, Ottawa, 15520.

Preface
Ian M. Thom
page 9

The Thing
that Makes a Picture
David P. Silcox
page 11

Milne and his
Contemporaries
Christine
Boyanoski
page 21

David Milne's
New York
Lora Senechal
Carney
page 37

David Milne

Boston Corners
Ian M. Thom
page 63

Creative Courage
Megan Bice
page 99

Milne and
Abstraction
François-Marc
Gagnon
page 131

The Late Work
Ian M. Thom
page 161

Chronology   209

Notes to the Essays   211

Notes to the Plates   218

Photo Credits   220

Index   221

3 THE OPEN STREAM. Alander, 10 February 1921. Watercolour over pencil on paper, 39.4 x 56.6.
Private collection.

■ This book and the exhibition from which it has grown are the products of a long period of study and work. The first Milne retrospective since 1967 (and only the second since his death), this exhibition seeks to introduce Milne's work to a new generation of Canadians and to re-assert his importance to Canadian painting. Although Milne's work has not been presented to the public in a comprehensive way for several years, he has not been absent from exhibitions, nor has his work been overlooked by scholars. The specialized studies of Rosemarie Tovell and John O'Brian have made important contributions to our knowledge of Milne's art. So too have the series of exhibitions held at the Mira Godard Gallery since 1976, and their accompanying catalogues.

All of the recent scholarship on Milne has been based on the invaluable research of David Milne Jr. His ongoing work on the catalogue raisonné, including an edition of Milne's writings, has been essential to the present project. So has his collaboration with David Silcox in compiling biographical material on David Milne. Some of the fruits of that research appear in this book in the form of the captions, which David Milne Jr has edited and compiled.

The titles of Milne's works have frequently been changed, by Milne himself and by others. Readers will find that some works are published here under titles quite different from those used in earlier exhibitions. The current titles, wherever possible, are titles given by Milne or derived from his writings and established by David Milne Jr during his work on the catalogue raisonné. Where

an alternate title exists, it is indicated in parentheses. All measurements are in centimetres, height before width.

For the sake of economy a number of abbreviations are used throughout the text – MFP for Milne Family Papers, MFC for Milne Family Collection, NAC for National Archives of Canada, NGC for National Gallery of Canada and MC for Massey College, University of Toronto. Bold figures in square brackets – [12], for example – refer to the numbered plates.

Milne remains one of the most astute commentators on his own work, and we have therefore often quoted his own words about his life and work. As much as possible, we have retained his spellings and the distinctive character of his prose, while correcting any gratuitous errors or confusing use of language. Milne was an extremely thoughtful man who expressed himself eloquently. He often revisited ideas in both his art and writings. Language and point of view differ in texts dealing with the same subject, and as Milne did not intend most of his writing for publication, there is no definitive text. Where varying texts have been quoted in this book, readers will discover subtle changes in Milne's thought and expression.

The essays published here are Milne studies, not individual chapters in a biography, nor is this the final word on Milne's art. Milne, like every great artist, speaks, and will continue to speak, differently to each of us. It is our hope that through this exhibition and book, the power of Milne's "creative courage" will be evident to many more Canadians.

Preface

Ian M. Thom

4 WINDOW. Palgrave, 1930. Oil on canvas, 56.3 x 71.8.
National Gallery of Canada, Ottawa, 15516.

■ In October 1934, after some weeks of reflection and writing drafts, David Milne dispatched a brave and remarkable letter to Alice and Vincent Massey. He offered to sell them his life's work, about a thousand paintings, for five dollars each. The Masseys had purchased a painting, *Window* [4], two years earlier for one hundred and seventy-five dollars from one of the few exhibitions to which Milne had sent work in the thirties and, since they were already known as art patrons, it was perhaps natural that he should write his unusual proposal to them. The letter was twenty-six pages long, illustrated with nine deft and elegant ink drawings. In it, Milne traced his life, chronologically and artistically, describing how he had developed his ideas and methods as an artist, and how he had made his way from rural Ontario to New York City, gained a proud measure of success there prior to the First World War, including exhibiting in the famous Armory Show, and finally, after subsequent mixed fortune, returned to Canada. A remarkable document about art, the letter is a matchless source of information about Milne's attitudes to painting, exhibiting, selling and appreciating pictures. Clearly he had reached a turning point from which, looking back over his life, he saw a commendable amount of achievement and of exhibition activity, but little recognition and less income. Ahead, he saw only obstacles to the only thing he wanted to do, which was to paint. If he could purchase a few years of painting time by selling what thus far had seemed unsaleable, he would be satisfied.

Here he was, about to turn fifty-three, in the midst of the Depression and almost penniless, recently separated from his wife, and living alone in a tiny, isolated, tarpaper shack on Six Mile Lake near Georgian Bay. Milne was virtually an unknown in Canada, having spent most of his adult life in the United States. Given the path that his life had taken, he did not have, at that point, a great deal more to risk by approaching the Masseys; and with assistance he would be able to paint productively for some years more. In fact, as fate would arrange, Milne was little more than half way through the span of his painting years, with a few more than twenty years behind him, and not quite twenty stretching out ahead. How did someone with so much talent, achievement and sheer perseverance not manage to do a little better for himself financially? What critical responses to his work might have contributed to these straitened circumstances?

Milne himself had an excuse or two, rationalizations perhaps, as to why he was where he was. To the Masseys, to whom he was, after all, making a sales pitch, he suggested that the very nature of his work, the development of themes and motifs over series of paintings, made them unsuitable for exhibiting casually: "they call for special exhibition methods," he wrote. Reviving a thought of some years earlier, he added that he had wanted to catalogue all his paintings carefully, relating the development from one to another and plotting the track of aesthetic concerns through different series. That was why, like J.M.W. Turner, he wanted to keep all his paintings together: collectively they explored more subtle and powerful aesthetic ideas and made a strong statement. He mentioned, further, that he had no money for frames or stretchers and, in any case, that nothing ever sold through exhibitions. Writing to his New York friend, mentor and supporter James Clarke, he imagined several other reasons. The first was that his paintings were small and did not stand out in exhibitions; nor, presumably, were they as attractive to potential buyers as larger paintings. Then, he thought that his work was not sufficiently realistic compared to that of other artists:

The Thing that Makes a Picture
David P. Silcox

there was no "story interest," no anecdote which people could use to relate the painting to something else and thus find a more "general appeal." And, finally, he believed that his work was neither academic nor modernistic, and thus had no point of reference to other work which people might know. These "marketing" deficiencies, he thought, made the sale of his paintings, unless someone knowledgeable was promoting them, nearly an impossibility.

All artists struggle, to varying degrees, with the conflict between the impulse which creates a work of art and the process which sells it for a price. For some artists, the commercial part of their lives is relatively easy to bear: they make arrangements in a businesslike way and detach themselves, as artists, from the process. For artists at the other extreme, all dealings with their works become painful and agonizing. They end up investing their creative energy in processes which, inevitably, raise troubling questions in their minds about worth, reputation, and artistic integrity. Milne was not initially a worrier, nor did he falter in believing in himself. But as years went by and he reached full middle age without achieving a modicum of steady success in sales or even a stable arrangement with a gallery which could sustain him at a modest level, he began to seek out ways to support himself. Without the bedrock support and unflagging encouragement of his friend and patron James Clarke, however, his life as an artist would doubtless have been put to even more severe tests.

Milne's first recorded public exhibition, with a pastel called *Classen Point Road*, was at the American Water Color Society in New York in the spring of 1909. Although he told the Masseys that he had begun exhibiting earlier, in 1907, references have been found only to one or two

student shows. Almost every year from 1910 until 1922, Milne showed his work with the New York and Philadelphia Water Color Clubs, and the American Water Color Society, often with several works in each exhibition. After he hit his full stride as an artist in mid-1911, he was practically a fixture in the New York art world. With a group of six artist friends, he helped to arrange an exhibition called *Contemporaries* in 1913. He showed at the renowned Montross Gallery where such important Americans as Walt Kuhn, Robert Henri, Charles Sheeler, Maurice Prendergast, William Glackens and Arthur Davies, and the Europeans Henri Matisse and Marcel Duchamp were regularly seen. In 1914, a handsome reproduction in the *New York Times* of the painting *Red* [5] from one of the Montross group shows was a telling indication of the stature Milne had achieved. He served on exhibition juries with George Luks, Alden Weir, Joseph Pennell, Arthur Crisp and other leading artists, and was on the Board of Control of the New York Water Color Club by the time he left the city in 1916. Milne had even held his own one-man show in his apartment in 1915, where he painted the walls black and, according to his wife, sold well.

In retrospect, the high point of Milne's New York career was the 1913 International Exhibition of Modern Art, or the Armory Show as it is familiarly called. Although Milne himself confessed that he and his fellow North Americans were largely ignored in the furor over the European selections, he was in company of the first rank. His two oils and three water colours were more than were allowed to such artists as Edward Hopper, Marguerite and William Zorach, or Joseph Stella. Milne was one of the few "American" artists whose work was chosen for the greatly condensed version of the Armory Show which went on from New York to Chicago. More

12

honour and attention came to him when he received a silver medal (Ernest Lawson got a gold) at San Francisco's Panama-Pacific Exposition in 1915, a vast West Coast emulation of the sprawling Armory Show. The one final fortress of acceptance, the National Academy of Design, accepted Milne's submission in 1915, though the compliment was qualified by hanging his painting, *Blue-Green, Black-Green* – probably *Hudson from Weehawken* [7] – "high up behind the door in the morgue."

In addition to all this attention, Milne was well-treated critically. The conservative critics, predictably, lumped him in with "extremists" like Maurice Prendergast, Walter Pach and William Zorach, and found his work "clever, if bilious," "a pictorial joke," or shuddered at his "raw colors." One now-forgotten artist, Clinton Peters, obviously gazing at "the nightmare" of Milne's *Columbus Circle* (now *Billboards* [26]), declared "there's one thing the cubists [who could have imagined Milne as a cubist!] have done ... they certainly have squared the circle." Amusingly, another critic called Milne a one-man "Circlist" school because "he represents a scene in Columbus Circle in a multitude of rings of paint."

But the perceptive and intelligent (and mostly anonymous) critics who understood the modernist movement, frequently and regularly singled Milne out as someone who was both original and distinctive, and whose work had power and freshness. According to the critic of the *New York American*, reviewing a Montross group show, both *Black* [6] and *Red* "have the charm of an individuality that is at once sensitive and virile." The *New York Times* critic wrote of Milne that he was an artist with "a genius for fashion. Not one in a thousand can spot a piece of paper as cleverly as he." In reviewing the American Water Color Society's annual show of 1914, one critic began by noting that there was "many an agreeable thing to show, but none more invigorating than David B. Milne's" submission, and he concluded that Milne's work was "always brilliant and beautiful." The *New York Sun* critic, threading his way reluctantly through the "crazy post-impressionists" of the New York Water Color Club's show, concluded that "the best essays in modernism ... were those of David B. Milne, whose color is vivid, yet pleasing and whose decorative bent is pronounced." Other critics at other times saw Milne's work as being poster-like, or schematic, or scientific, as they mistook a "lack of drawing" or of modelling as a fault. Milne's aesthetic intention was quite different, and the *New York Times* critic caught it quite well as early as 1911:

Then there is the Neo-Impressionist, or his successor, who divides his tones, uses pure color according to the laws of complementary hues and optics, and who limits his blots of pigment to a size definitely proportioned to the area of the space he has to cover. Signac and Seurat were leaders in this school twenty years ago, and Mr Milne and his companions in this particular art form owe much to their experiments.... Although the picture [Black and White, 1911] depends upon the relation of the spots of flat color for its effect, Mr Milne has not disregarded linear means. Some of his figures are boldly and richly outlined in color and the rhythm of these flexible lines contributes to the charm of the composition. The whole is very brilliant, very animated, conceived with vigor and executed with dexterity.

Among artists, Milne was clearly regarded as a contender, creative and gifted; among the leading critics, a force to reckon with. Yet he did not rise further. Just when he might have reached a new plateau, he left New York City and, inexplicably or perhaps as a consequence, never managed to gain a wider acceptance. He was never more than

David B. Milne . . . maps out his pattern with scientific accuracy. In the subjects shown at the present exhibition science is all that stands between the old and the new. How many times have we not seen that slim girl in a library, pots of flowers on the window bench, and the light falling in warm patches on the floor and furniture. But Mr Milne has made himself master of the art of patterning and builds up his blocks of color as precisely as the modern doctor diagrams your heart action.
— New York Times, 1914

5 R E D . West Saugerties, 1914. Oil on canvas, 50.8 x 55.6. Milne Family Collection.

14

Pretty much a working out of the values problem, which of course goes way back — the interest in values apart from color. You may remember one of Patsy reading a newspaper against the light of a window in the black room at Park Avenue. Indian red and cerulean blue in it. The window white and the values kept away down. Another one of Patsy in Mrs Myers store at W. Saugerties similar [Red, plate 5]. . . . That was a value problem.
Milne to Clarke,
Jan–Feb 1928 [NAC]

6 BLACK. New York, 1914. Oil on canvas, 51.9 x 61.9.
McMichael Canadian Art Collection, Gift of the Founders, Robert and Signe McMichael, 1966.16.23.

7 HUDSON FROM WEEHAWKEN. New York c. 1914. Oil on canvas, 50.8 x 61.
National Gallery of Canada, Ottawa, 16428.

a candidate for the kind of social and financial success that, for example, Childe Hassam enjoyed, though of the two Milne was considered by some critics to have the superior talent. Was he too thin-skinned, too unwilling to elbow his way forward, or was he genuinely too diffident to succeed in an abrasive market, or was his work just different enough not to catch on more readily?

One factor was decisive for Milne, at least as he looked back: he did not sell enough work to support himself without recourse to commercial artwork. Illustrating for magazines, as he did when he first went to New York, or making showcards for store windows was what kept him going. In his little memoir to the Masseys, he claimed that only two works ever sold out of public exhibitions. This was an obvious understatement, but it pointed at a truth. After Milne moved to Boston Corners in upstate New York in 1916, and again when he returned there after the First World War, he could not elicit interest from the dealers who had shown his works earlier. Clarke, a successful commercial artist, made occasional purchases for friends and had his firm commission two oil paintings. A number more sold from a 1922 exhibition at Cornell University, and six watercolours were purchased by the National Gallery of Canada in 1924 for less than one hundred and fifty dollars. Otherwise Milne sold no work for sixteen years. In the midst of this lack of success, an odd benefactor appeared: the military.

One of the fulfilling experiences of Milne's life, from both a personal and artistic point of view, occurred after he decided to enlist in the Canadian Army toward the end of 1917. He trained in Toronto in early 1918 and went to England in the fall, just in time for the Armistice. By one of the happiest circumstances of his life,

he secured an appointment as a war artist and spent nine months painting in England and France, being given all the supplies he needed, having the freedom to paint what he wanted, and being looked after as far as food, transport, shelter and clothes (uniforms) were concerned. He painted well over a hundred watercolours, and was encouraged and praised at every turn, in one instance being compared favourably by P.G. Konody, a leading London critic and advisor to Lord Beaverbrook, to Vincent van Gogh. Milne's work was included in several later exhibitions of war art, but his watercolours, though of unquestioned merit, were constantly upstaged by other artists' larger, "more substantial" oils which dealt with the action of war whereas his dealt, for the most part, with its aftermath. Still, he thought that this coherent and dramatic achievement might give him an entrée to his native land by providing credentials to launch his career in Canada. He didn't count on the phlegmatic Canadian character. No one called or wrote to offer him a position or an opportunity, and he returned to New York State.

In the Adirondacks in the summer of 1921, Milne met a Norwegian named Christian Midjo, an art teacher at Cornell University, who invited Milne to exhibit his watercolours there in 1922. This led to a few sales, but reviews of the exhibition, if there were any, have not been found. At the same time, Milne was rebuffed by commercial dealers in New York City, for reasons we do not know, and by the societies which had been showing his work since 1910. His reputation in the United States, rather than expanding, seemed to be contracting and this may have prompted his determination to return to Canada.

Milne made a foray to Ottawa in the fall of 1923, for a time leaving his wife, with whom relations were by now somewhat strained. He threw himself into a flurry of initiatives which were going to make him known. He proposed to start an art school or at least give lessons, but that plan fizzled out quickly. The Ottawa Art Club invited him to give a three-hour exhibition and a lecture, but there were no sales. At the National Gallery he found sympathetic curators who greatly admired his painting and recommended him to others. Although they were acquiring other contemporary artists' works at twelve to fifteen hundred dollars each, they bought six superb watercolours from Milne at twenty to thirty dollars each, with a discount for quantity purchase. This may have been Milne's asking price, but it did not make him financially solvent.

But the nadir of the whole initiative to become a known Canadian artist came when the Art Association of Montreal (later the Montreal Museum of Fine Arts) held a retrospective of his work in watercolour early in 1924 and neither bought nor sold one of the nearly one hundred paintings shown (three thousand dollars could have purchased everything). Nor was success any better at subsequent exhibitions at the Arts Club of Montreal; at Hart House, University of Toronto; or later in the spring at either the Arts and Letters Club or the Ontario College of Art, where J.E.H. MacDonald arranged to show his works. There were no takers, MacDonald wrote, and only "a great deal of silent wondering from the critics." Dismayed by the Montreal experience, Milne retreated to the Adirondacks to build a house and tea room and to run a ski-jump teahouse. He was there for five more years.

Milne's career did not develop significantly in the Adirondacks, for painting was often desultory and there were no exhibitions. Milne returned to Ontario again in 1929, anxious to get away from his building project and his wife. He spent the summer in Temagami and a winter in Weston, a Toronto suburb, then settled in Palgrave for three years and finally moved on, alone, to Six Mile Lake. Though his painting went well in Temagami and Palgrave, attempts to earn his way or to be noticed were not successful. Only the chance sale to the Masseys provided any cheer during what was a bleak time for him financially. Not only was Milne not adept at promoting himself, he did not know how to go about either bringing his works to market or selling them to those who could afford them. Perhaps he should follow Cézanne's example, he suggested to Harry McCurry at the National Gallery, and leave his paintings standing in the fields where he painted them. As he remarked to the Masseys, "exhibiting and painting are quite different departments" and he was only good at the latter. The route of the public or society exhibition was not a straight road to riches.

The Masseys' response to Milne's proposal was an offer to buy three hundred paintings for fifteen hundred dollars, and Milne agreed. The Masseys then decided to give a few to museums, and to arrange exhibitions in commercial galleries in Toronto (Mellors Galleries), Ottawa (Jas. Wilson & Co.), and Montreal (Scott and Sons). Further, they wanted Milne to have some of the profit that would accumulate after all costs, including the original purchase cost, had been met. With some of the proceeds, they told Milne, they would give further support to Canadian artists. Milne hesitated only briefly. The total amount of money did not buy him the time he had hoped for, and he was not at all pleased about splitting up the body work he had proposed to keep intact. But he could hardly be against helping Canadian art and artists, and the money got him out of a jam.

With the Masseys' support, connections and energy, Milne rapidly became more widely

18

known. Donald Buchanan, later a curator at the National Gallery, was commissioned by the Masseys to visit Milne, and he wrote glowingly of Milne's restrained and unique paintings in newspapers, *Canadian Art, Canadian Forum* and *Saturday Night*. With his recent exposure to French art, Buchanan found a key to Milne's work that was both astute and accurate. He described it as having "the bitter tang, the quick dry vitality, of French vermouth." Other art critics were just as laudatory, if not more so. Graham McInnes began his long and steady adulation of Milne with: "Of Mr Milne I find it difficult to speak with moderation, for he has made me see in the Canadian landscape a spirit whose existence I had never suspected, and he has completely upset any provisional classification of Canadian painting which I had begun to make in my own mind." Pearl McCarthy, in the *Mail and Empire*, wrote of Milne's debut at the Mellors Galleries that his work was "an extremely serious matter," and "stingingly sincere." She said his paintings were "a force to be reckoned with in Canadian art." The critics in Ottawa and Montreal echoed the same enthusiasm, and Milne's star indeed began to rise. Other artists, like Carl Schaefer, were complimentary, and sales were brisk at last.

But unknown to Milne, the Masseys had made a deal to split profits with Mellors both for their Milnes and for Milne's current production, which they had asked him to send along, presuming the same five dollars a canvas. Paintings sold for modest prices, at the Masseys' request, varying initially from twenty-five to one hundred and fifty dollars. By 1938 the Masseys had recouped their initial investment, been reimbursed a further five hundred and fifty dollars they had advanced to Milne, had all their framing and shipping paid, had covered all gallery expenses and commissions, and had sold or given a number of paintings to friends which were not reported or calculated as promised. Things were not helped much by the patronizing attitude of the Mellors Galleries to Milne's work, nor by the blunt references to the kind of subject matter that was or was not saleable. Milne, in frustration and desperation, finally brought in a lawyer to extricate himself. Even when he seemed to succeed, penury kept dogging his heels.

Out of this chaos which, nevertheless, catapulted Milne to prominence, two quite different and wonderful guardian angels miraculously emerged: Douglas Duncan and Kathleen Pavey. Duncan had learned of Milne's first exhibition at Mellors from Alan Jarvis, a student at the University of Toronto, and they both sought Milne out at Six Mile Lake. When the Mellors/Massey arrangement collapsed, Duncan stepped in and became Milne's agent and dealer. Until Milne's death fifteen years later, Duncan showed his work regularly, promoted it, photographed it, catalogued it, and sold it. In the company of such artists as Paul-Emile Borduas and Harold Town, among the many whom Duncan introduced to the Toronto art world, Milne became a respected name in Canadian art, and was considered the dean of Canadian painters in watercolour. Duncan became what Milne had always needed, someone who understood his work intuitively and well, and who did nearly everything for him that his professional life required. And that, in turn, became a problem during Milne's last few years. Duncan's well-known procrastination, combined with his absolute control over Milne's work and finances, finally caused a rupture in their relationship. Once again, Milne stood unprotected and at a disadvantage. Consequences were forestalled only by Milne's illness and death. Nevertheless, Duncan organized the first retrospective of Milne's work for the National Gallery

DAVID P. SILCOX

of Canada in 1956, when Alan Jarvis was its Director.

Kathleen Pavey literally blew into Milne's little Six Mile Lake bay in a storm in 1938 and eventually became Milne's second wife. Her support and companionship helped to settle Milne's later years. Their child, David, born in 1941 when Milne was fifty-nine, brought an element into Milne's life that inspired a steady flow of delightful, complex and masterful works, mostly in watercolour. Despite the stress of wartime rationing, a meagre income (Milne never earned more than twelve to fifteen hundred dollars in a year after the Massey sale), and continuing pressure from Milne's first wife, who needed money and had difficulty accepting the separation of years before, Milne enjoyed a decade or more of good painting until illness impeded his last few years.

Milne's work, since his death nearly forty years ago, has steadily gained in stature, in value and in price. Yet Milne – in life always somewhat apart as an artist, whether by choice, or by character or by default – has remained relatively unknown to the general public. What he has been, unquestionably, is the quintessential painters' painter. Perhaps only Tom Thomson and J.W. Morrice are as highly regarded by as many other artists as Milne was and is. The reason is that his work is about the act of painting and of experiencing art. He cared chiefly about whether anyone got an aesthetic thrill from a painting, something as sharp as an electric charge. For Milne, that was really all painting, or any aesthetic experience, was ever about. "The thing that 'makes' a picture" he wrote, "is the thing that 'makes' dynamite – compression. It isn't a fire in the grass; it is an explosion." Commerce in paintings was incidental and tangential to Milne's fundamental experience of painting or looking at painting and to the experience he expected others to get from painting. And that may be why, like Vincent van Gogh, with whom he felt a strong empathy, Milne did not care much if anyone owned his work, but cared very much if his work could touch someone profoundly.

Milne and his Contemporaries

Christine Boyanoski

David Milne's career was split almost equally between the United States and Canada. Born near Paisley, Ontario, in 1882, he moved to New York in 1903. It was not until 1929 that he settled once more in Canada, remaining in Ontario until his death in 1953. He is still little known south of the border, despite the more than twenty productive years he spent in the United States,[1] and Canada has rightly claimed him as a native son. However, Milne's place among his contemporaries is still in the process of being evaluated. Does his work bear any characteristics which would identify it as distinctly Canadian, American or North American, and where does he "fit" in relation to other artists of his day?

Milne originally left his rural home for New York City as a matter of "gravitation of the periphery to the centre,"[2] to pursue training in the area of commercial art. While he could not have been aware of it at the time, New York was soon to become the centre of modernist art activity in North America, largely through the combined influence of Alfred Stieglitz's Photo-Secession Gallery (known as "291"), which began showing the work of avant-garde painters and photographers in 1905; the Armory Show of 1913; and a number of galleries which promoted the cause of modern art after 1913. As John O'Brian has pointed out, New York was the only city on the North American continent at that time where Milne could have gained exposure to the art which would have an enduring impact on his own life's work.[3]

But Milne did not stay at the "centre." In 1916, he and his wife left New York and took up residence in the small community of Boston Corners in the Lower Berkshires, which had a history of attracting artists.[4] It proved to be his ideal painting place, one against which other locales would be measured for many years to come.[5] From then on, Milne spent little time in cities. (Although he moved to Toronto in 1939, he had already described that place as "an Old Testament city," "city of 'me and mine'," and returned to the country in 1940.) Instead, he sought out areas where he could be in direct contact with his subject matter (provided most often by nature), and where he could live cheaply, thus free to devote most of his time to painting.

Art historian Karen Wilkin has commented that as Milne retreated to increasingly remote places, he "retreated from the modernism of his early work."[6] She then concedes that rather than a retreat from modernism, his development may perhaps indicate the "gradual emergence of his mystical side" rooted in his admiration for the nineteenth century American naturalist and writer Henry David Thoreau (1817–1862). Finally, she admits that even this view may not be entirely accurate. What Wilkin and John O'Brian, whom she quotes, see as contradictions in Milne's work signify what was, in fact, a highly personal synthesis of nineteenth- and twentieth-century influences, in both stylistic and philosophical terms. Removal from direct contact with the frenetic art scene that was New York in 1915 permitted Milne's painting to develop naturally and without outside pressure, as Milne himself noted in his unpublished autobiography.

The benefits of working at the "periphery" have been recently examined, notably at the International Congress of the History of Art held in Washington in 1986. In an essay entitled "Some Values of Artistic Periphery," by Jan Bialostocki, *periphery* is defined as "an area where various influences mix and merge and where no one of them obtains decisive superiority; that allows the artists of the peripheral regions to make the choice to develop the independently chosen ele-

8 5 TREES AND DOME. New York, 1915.
Black ink over graphite on gampi tissue, 40.3 x 55.8.
Private collection.

9 LARGE TREE. New York, 1915. Gouache on gampi
tissue, 40 x 55.4. Milne Family Collection.

ments and to create out of various influences an art autonomous and original."[7]

Had Milne remained in New York City, the demands of daily life and the weight of prevailing influences might well have inhibited the development of what turned out to be a highly original art, one imbued with what he himself termed "creative courage." For example, the paintings he executed in 1915, just before leaving the city, are closely related to black-and-white pen-and-ink drawings he was doing at the time which in turn seem to have been influenced by the principle of "notan" demonstrated in Arthur Wesley Dow's highly influential art-school text, *Composition*.

Judging from these drawings, of which *Large Tree*, 1915 [9], is an example, Milne was probably reading Dow that year.[8] The drawings, of which only twenty-four are extant, closely resemble exercises in "notan" (massing of forms in two values, black and white) and are significant for the considerable impact they had on his work. Milne criticized the late New York paintings as "mannered, heavy, spotty," blaming the influence of his black and white brush drawings.[9] Once he distanced himself from New York City, Milne was able to digest the significance of these drawings, and integrate what he learned into his work.[10] Colour values – that is, their equivalence on a tonal scale of black to white – and the role he assigned to these values in his compositions were to occupy Milne for many years to come.

Milne was not alone in quitting the big city. Other progressive artists, notably of Alfred Stieglitz's stable, also carried out much of their creative work in locations removed from New York, while maintaining a connection with it, sometimes through Stieglitz himself. He helped these artists considerably by refusing personal remuneration for the services he provided them, especially by exposing their work to the public in his gallery. John Marin (1870–1953), Arthur Dove (1880–1946) and Georgia O'Keeffe (1887–1986) in particular needed remoteness, and a closeness to nature not provided by life in the city. Marin lived in Cliffside, New Jersey; Dove, for a time in Westport, Connecticut; and O'Keeffe, having made her first trip to the Southwest in 1917, spent her summers in New Mexico from 1929 on.[11]

It is not unreasonable to consider Milne in the company of these American painters, for his work relates more closely to theirs than to most other art of his generation. They were part of the avant-garde at the time of the Armory Show in 1913, and Milne could have seen the work of Dove and Marin (whom he apparently met in 1910)[12] at "291" before leaving the city. It was work that adhered to modernist tenets, while at the same time maintaining a close relationship with nature. This too describes the essence of Milne's art – a romantic formalism. The differences between their work and that of Milne have to do with the presence of an emotional or symbolic element in the American work which is absent in the Canadian's more purely formalist expression. Milne was not interested in extracting meanings which lay hidden in nature's forms and patterns, nor in expressing an emotional response to those forms and patterns, but in relaying to the viewer the charge he himself received upon contact with certain motifs in nature which excited his keen visual sense.

Lacking a benefactor like Stieglitz,[13] and with relatively few opportunities to exhibit his work, Milne paid a greater price than his contemporaries for the isolation he needed. Boston Corners had initially seemed attractive because of its easy access by train to New York, but he found framing and shipping too expensive to send work to the city for exhibition on a regular basis. Moreover,

10 PORCH OF SUMMER CAMP. 1921. Brush drawing on paper, 38 x 41.
Art Gallery of Ontario, Toronto, 59/60.

he was disinclined to exhibit, admitting that his work was difficult to show. Not only did he work on a relatively small scale (unsuitable for large rooms in public galleries), but the non-representational nature of the pictures themselves limited their popularity. And since his working method was such that the formal aspects of each picture developed logically out of themes dealt with in preceding ones, an exhibition representing an entire year's work might show little variety to an eye unused to subtle variations in formal themes.[14]

Milne exhibited his work occasionally in the United States in the 1920s: at the Montross Gallery in New York City; with the Philadelphia Water Color Club, the Boston Water Color Society, and the American Federation of Arts; and at Cornell University in 1922. The Carnegie Institute and Corcoran Gallery shows were not open to him (presumably because of his Canadian citizenship), which limited him to the less rigid watercolour societies.

Milne was relatively unknown in Canada when he arrived back in this country, although he had exhibited in a Canadian context on more than one occasion before 1929. J.E.H. MacDonald (1873–1932), a member of the Group of Seven, and an editor of *Canadian Forum* in the 1920s, published one of Milne's drawings, *Porch of Summer Camp*, 1921 [**10**], in the journal in July 1924, around the time that an exhibition of his work was held in Toronto, probably at the Arts and Letters Club. Concerning critical response to the show, MacDonald wrote to Milne:

There was considerable interest shown in the drawings, but a great deal of silent wondering from the critics. The artist chaps generally felt the merits of design, freedom and originality, whether they approved the method or not. As far as I am concerned you are the doctor, and you

have my blessing, even though I would like to see something more of the why and wherefores of your methods if you were here.[15]

Examples of Milne's work were also included in the British Empire Exhibition, Wembley, England, in 1924 and 1925 (where critical reaction focussed on the "school of landscape painters racy of the soil," to which he did not belong); at Hart House, University of Toronto; with "The Ottawa Group" early in 1924; and at the Art Association of Montreal (a one-man show initiated by his wife). The first Special Exhibition of Canadian Art in 1926 at the National Gallery of Canada also contained one watercolour by Milne.

On his return, Milne wasted no time before attempting to break into the world of exhibiting in Toronto, and in February 1930 was quite optimistic about his prospects of doing so. He showed four works at the Annual Exhibition of the Ontario Society of Artists (OSA) in March – *Painting Place*, 1930 [**2**], and three drypoints, and was stimulated to see his work in new surroundings. He also pursued the possibility of showing with the Group of Seven in March of that year, wishing to increase his range of exhibiting possibilities, and curious to see how his work would look in their company. He was told, however, that it was a private show; pictures by those outside the group were included by invitation only.[16]

After 1930, Milne showed regularly with the OSA, also with the Canadian Society of Graphic Arts, the Canadian Group of Painters, the Canadian Society of Painters in Water Colour – in short, all the major exhibiting societies based in Toronto, which from Milne's vantage point in Weston, Palgrave, Six Mile Lake, Uxbridge, and finally, Bancroft, Ontario, constituted the "centre" of art activity in Canada. Through an arrangement with the Masseys in 1934, five exhibitions of his work were held at the Mellors Galleries, Toronto, until Douglas Duncan became his agent in 1938 and began to show the work at the Picture Loan Society.

How has Milne's work been received by Canadian audiences? According to MacDonald, it met with some confusion in 1924. When he was first "discovered" by a larger Canadian audience a decade later, Milne was made a part of the Canadian mythology. By "Canadian mythology," I mean the image of the independent artist/adventurer who braves the wilds in search of subject matter. The early topographical artists were the earliest examples, and the tradition has carried on into this century with Tom Thomson and the Group of Seven. These romantic figures are perhaps the closest we Canadians come to having heroes.[17] Donald Buchanan (1908–1966) was one of the first to write about Milne's work after visiting the artist at Six Mile Lake in the fall of 1934. The titles of Buchanan's articles introduced Milne as "An Artist who Lives in the Woods," and "An Artist in a Forest Hut,"[18] although the content of these writings and later ones aligned him with modern French painters, particularly Matisse. *Telegram* columnist Kenneth Wells described Milne as the "Log Cabin Artist," the "man who had the courage to answer the call of the wilds," and as one who might fill the void left by the death of Tom Thomson in 1917.[19]

In 1935 and 1936, Graham McInnes (1912–1970) and Alan Jarvis (1915–1972) commented on the fact that Milne was being compared to Thomson. Jarvis – a talented art student who later became director of the National Gallery of Canada – immediately sloughed off the comparison as if it belittled Milne, and seemed compelled to defend the latter's choice for "living alone on the shores of a deserted Muskoka lake." McInnes, an enlightened art critic, sought to explain the

comparison: in his opinion, the two artists were alike in their "great understanding of and sympathy for the North country, and in their intensity," but differed in the way they realized this intensity.[20]

While placing Milne in this romantic tradition does not take us far in evaluating his work in the context of his contemporaries, the relevance of Thomson should not be overlooked. In the first place, by the mid-thirties, it was felt that art in English Canada was in need of revitalization, which "another Thomson" might provide. Several publications on Thomson appeared in the 1930s, notably Blodwen Davies' *Paddle and Palette: The Story of Tom Thomson*, an unashamedly romantic version of the artist's life. Davies writes:

Through the story of painting in Canada there stalks a tall, lean trailsman, with his sketchbox and his paddle, an artist and dreamer who made the wilderness his cloister and there worshipped nature in her secret moods.... Tom Thomson, the legend, is one of the most vital influences in the creative life of Canada.[21]

Davies published a second book, *A Study of Tom Thomson: The Story of a Man who Looked for Beauty and Truth in the Wilderness* (1935), which Milne knew, and in 1937, the twentieth anniversary of Thomson's death, Ryerson Press published A.H. Robson's *Tom Thomson: Painter of our North Country*. Also that year, the Mellors Galleries mounted an exhibition of Thomson's work, with a catalogue written by J.M. MacCallum. Of Thomson, MacCallum wrote: "The north country enthralled him, body and soul. He began to paint that he might express the emotion the country inspired in him; all the moods and passions, all the sombreness and all the glory of colour...."

This romanticism aside, it is true that Milne himself admired Thomson's work, but for its formal qualities, not for the emotion based on associations that it aroused in others. He admired *The West Wind*, 1917, on more than one occasion, feeling that Thomson was the only Canadian painter who was influenced in his use of colour and line by Canadian subjects. It is interesting that he should connect formalist concerns with subject matter here, or enter into a discussion of "Canadian art" at all, for he maintained that subject matter was irrelevant, and the issue of nationalism did not concern him. He wrote: "Your Canadian art apparently for now, at least, went down in Canoe Lake. Tom Thomson still stands as *the* Canadian painter, harsh, brilliant, brittle, uncouth, not only most Canadian but most creative. How the few things of his stick in my mind."[22] He acknowledged Thomson as the "daddy of Canadian painting today," and while recognizing the latter's debt to Gauguin, felt that he had made something of his own out of it. Milne admired his lack of perfection, for he was critical of clever draftsmanship which was "neither emotion nor creation."[23] He saw in Thomson's personal use of colour and line an effective expression of the motif before him (in this case the rugged landscape of the Canadian Shield).

It was against this background that Milne was also received by some critics of Canadian art abroad. Reviews of the significant travelling show entitled *A Century of Canadian Art*, first held at the Tate Gallery, London, in 1938, repeatedly referred to Milne as living in "a remote hut on Georgian Bay, working out artistic theories," and again placed him in the tradition of "artist adventurers" like Paul Kane and Tom Thomson. Others, however, like Eric Newton, critic of the London *Sunday Times*, observed Milne's independence from the "Canadian tradition," noting the individuality and originality evident in the

small sampling of four works which stood out in such marked contrast to the work of his fellow artists.[24] *Window*, 1930 [4], *Painting Place*, 1930 [2], a watercolour entitled *Candy Box*, and *The Cross Chute*, 1938 [11], were shown. Writing a few months later in *Canadian Forum*, Newton referred to Milne as the most important tributary from the main stream of Canadian art – "the most individual of the Canadian painters both in his vision and in his method...."[25]

When in 1952 Canada was invited to participate for the first time at the Venice Biennale, paintings were selected to demonstrate the variety in Canadian art, and symbolically, a receptivity to cosmopolitan concerns. Pictures which reflected parochialism (nationalism and regionalism) would not have presented an appropriate image of a nation anxious to play a role on the international scene. Eight works by Milne were included, along with those of Goodridge Roberts (1904–1974), Emily Carr (1871–1945), and Alfred Pellan (1906–1988), all of whom may be considered artistic individualists.[26]

Just as squeezing Milne into the Canadian art myth impedes a clear evaluation of his art, grouping him with other so-called "independent artists" is equally unhelpful. The Montreal newspaper *La Presse* observed in 1935 that his work was "ni canadienne, ni française, ni anglaise." He is usually described in terms of what he wasn't, particularly in relation to the Group of Seven, by whose influence he remained untouched. McInnes commented that both Milne and the Group were "romantics," but whereas for Milne this applied only to his choice of subject matter, for the latter it extended to method, technique and aesthetic precepts.[27] It was natural that there should be some common ground since they were contemporaries, and their formative years were similarly spent absorbing the lessons of post-im-

11 THE CROSS CHUTE. Six Mile Lake, 1938. Watercolour over pencil on paper, 36.9 x 53.3.
National Gallery of Canada, Ottawa, 16430.

28

pressionism. From the start, however, they sprang from different branches of the same trunk: for the Group, it was Van Gogh and Gauguin; for Milne, Cézanne and Matisse.[28]

This tendency to group Milne with other "independents" has become a tradition. J. Russell Harper, who referred to Milne as "profoundly out of tune with the spirit of the Group of Seven," placed him in the company of Emily Carr and W.J. Wood, since they shared "some of the more personal approaches which filled areas of art untouched by the Group of Seven." More recently, in their writings and presentations of Milne in the two major collections of Canadian art under their care, curators Dennis Reid (Art Gallery of Ontario) and Charles Hill (National Gallery of Canada) have placed him in the company of L. LeMoine FitzGerald, the "independent" painter from Winnipeg.[29] While it is true that Milne and FitzGerald both needed some degree of solitude and contact with nature, they were far apart in many theoretical aspects, and this distance ultimately manifested itself in their artistic expression. Furthermore, Milne would have seen little affinity between them, for he was of the opinion that FitzGerald's work lacked the most important quality in art, "creative courage," since "he has got too far along in craftsmanship, without saying anything of his own to be helpful. If they had never been done by anyone else his pictures would be masterpieces, but that is the point, if they lack creative courage, they lack all."[30]

Why, in spite of the fact that his art bears some affinity to that of his Canadian and American contemporaries, does Milne continue to defy neat categorization? The answer can probably be found in the great importance he personally placed on originality, the distaste he felt for copying (which he often observed in the work of others), and his highly eclectic approach to art,

bred of independent thinking at the peripheries of the art world. This approach permitted him to incorporate seemingly antithetical elements into his personal philosophy of art. He could accept certain formalist tenets as expressed by early twentieth-century modernist critics like Clive Bell and Roger Fry, while at the same time appreciating aspects of the writings of nineteenth-century critic John Ruskin, and absorbing the philosophy of Thoreau. He could also admire the aesthetic qualities inherent in the work of artists as diverse as Piero di Cosimo (1462–1521), El Greco (1541–1614), Claude Monet (1840–1926), J.W. Morrice (1865–1924) and A.Y. Jackson (1882–1974), or praise the critical writings of certain others while finding nothing of value in the art they produced (Bertram Brooker, 1888–1955, W.S. Maxwell 1874–1952).[31] All of this, including his personal philosophy, which was clearly formulated by the mid-1930s, is revealed in his unpublished letters. These must be seen in relation to the work itself, however, for as Milne advised Donald Buchanan, "Never believe what an artist says, except on canvas – not even on canvas. He probably isn't making statements he is just feeling and mumbling to himself...."[32]

Taken on their own, Milne's words might lead one to believe that his art would look more abstract (removed from nature) than it actually does. *White, the Waterfall* [**58**], painted in the Lower Berkshires in the spring of 1921, and a picture he kept with him for years, was described by Milne in strictly formal terms. He wrote: "This is the open and shut motive, simplification by worked over and blank areas. A patiently worked, faulty picture, but it has a 'kick' that I have not been able to increase."[33] This painting was done at a time when Milne, leading a "Thoreau-esque" life in an isolated hut on Alander Mountain, was struggling to obtain in oil the same freedom and simplicity that he had achieved in his wartime watercolours. His formal means – colour and line – were sparingly used, with colour directed specifically at making the arrangement of shapes legible.

Milne's guiding principle of instant legibility through aesthetic economy was gradually woven into a philosophy centred upon the notions of "aesthetic emotion" (also referred to as "aesthetic feeling" and "aesthetic quickening"), a term he picked up from reading Clive Bell's *Art* in 1920, and "creative courage," or originality. In order that the artist's most intense feeling and quickest thought (aesthetic emotion before the motif) be conveyed to the viewer, speed of execution was an important factor. He stated, "The less the expenditure of aesthetic means (color and line), the greater the power of the picture."[34] As Milne's work progressed, he pushed the notion of speed almost to the point of full abstraction. Around 1932, Milne began to draw on the canvas (he defined painting as "drawing made more readable"), later completing the picture indoors, whereas previously he had completed it in one sitting before the motif. The drawing served to jog the memory and carried the sense of the picture: "Everything is there – all your shape." Colour was added to increase its legibility and convey the aesthetic emotion with increased rapidity. The pictures in which he pushed this notion to the extreme were done between 1935 and 1937. Of them he wrote:

The most successful ones seem to be the ones that are caught the quickest, and are farthest from the realistic. The idea is to get a strong kick from the subject, and let the putting of it on the canvas take care of itself. Have the thing strongly enough fired in your mind, then grab your brushes and just fall over the canvas.[35]

Like many of his generation, Milne never crossed the line into full abstraction. His rough pencilled line, no matter how rapidly it swept the canvas, always conveys the impression of something the artist actually saw and experienced. In a letter to Alice Massey concerning his "figure" paintings, he affirmed, "I don't go outside my own experience for material...."[36] This is also true of the American modernist painter John Marin, whose sensibility and stylistic expression often run parallel to Milne's. Compare, for instance, Marin's *Deer Isle, Maine, Movement No. 21, The Sea and Pertaining Thereto*, a watercolour of 1927, and Milne's *Track on the Ice*, 1937 [12].

That one is a watercolour, the other an oil is of little consequence here, for the looseness which characterizes *Track on the Ice* Milne translated into watercolour when he returned to using that medium in 1937 (exemplified by *The Cross Chute* [11]).[37] Both artists have chosen a high vantage point, so that the landscape spreads out before them like a tilted-up drawing board. Upon a sketchily drawn armature, colour has been added to give meaning to the structure. In Marin's case, the colour is more independent of line, and consequently plays a larger role in enhancing the meaning of the picture than it does in the Milne.

Marin, like Milne, developed a highly original art by combining a variety of artistic tendencies of his day – fauvism, expressionism, cubism – but also like Milne, his modernist leanings were balanced by a deep appreciation for nature established in youth. A statement made about Marin shortly after his death could equally be applied to Milne: "[Marin's] style, idiomatic and modern, expresses the long American love affair with the land. Though its condensed images and visual metaphor may occasionally remind us of a contemporary poet like E.E. Cummings, the spirit

Far left: Tom Thomson. **The West Wind**. 1917. Oil on canvas, 121 x 138. Art Gallery of Ontario, Toronto, 784.

Near left: Arthur G. Dove. **Waterfall**. 1925. Oil on masonite, 25 x 20. Phillips Collection, Washington, DC, 0586.

John Marin. **Movement, Sea and Pertaining Thereto, Deer Isle, Maine**. 1927. Watercolor on paper, 42 x 57. Metropolitan Museum of Art, New York, 49.70.138.

12 TRACK ON THE ICE. 1937. Oil on canvas, 31.4 x 36.3. Art Gallery of Ontario, Toronto, 51/89.

harks back to the institutions of a Thoreau or the freedom of a Whitman."[38]

In 1928 Marin wrote:

Seems to me the true artist must perforce go from time to time to the elemental big forms – Sky, Sea, Mountain, Plain, – and those things pertaining thereto, to sort of re-true himself up, to recharge the battery. For these big forms have everything. But to express these, you have to love these, to be a part of these in sympathy.[39]

Similarly Milne noted that while writing or painting with one hand, he had to have someone, "mostly nature," holding the other,[40] and wrote in his autobiographical letter to Vincent and Alice Massey in 1934: "Your direction is always being changed by your contact with nature"; and "The painter gets an impression from some phase of nature...."[41] This held true, no matter how spare his expression.

The influence of Thoreau and poet Walt Whitman (1819–1892) on late nineteenth- and twentieth-century artists has been demonstrated in an exhibition entitled *Henry David Thoreau as a Source for Artistic Inspiration*, which included work by twentieth-century artists Charles Burchfield (1893–1967), Marsden Hartley (1877–1943), N.C. Wyeth (1882–1945), and others. Upon re-reading *Walden* in 1920, Milne, as we have seen, felt compelled to spend a winter in a hut in the Berkshire Hills in emulation of Thoreau. In Canada, J.E.H. MacDonald, one of the original members of the Group of Seven, was also drawn to the writings of Thoreau. According to his son, whom he had named Thoreau (1901–1989), the elder MacDonald felt *Walden* "contained more ideas for weight than other books" and in the 1920s lectured on Whitman.[42]

By way of contrast, another of Milne's contemporaries in the United States, Arthur Dove (1880–1946), whose starting point was also nature, *did* cross over into full abstraction. Dove, like Milne, felt that the " 'first flash' of an idea gives its most vivid sensation...," but where he differed from Milne was in trying "to put down the spirit of the idea as it comes out.... It is the form that the idea takes in the imagination rather than the form as it exists outside."[43] It was the spirit of the thing that Dove sought to convey in his *Waterfall*, 1925, painted four years after Milne's version, where nature is merely the point of departure in his choice of "form motive." Dove wrote: "Why not make things look like nature? Because I do not consider that important and it is my nature to make them this way. To me it is perfectly natural. They exist in themselves, as an object does in nature."[44]

Milne's last exhibition with the Mellors Galleries was held in January 1938 and featured recent pictures. Among the forty-four works were *Red Nasturtiums* [120] and *New Shelf* [108]. In the way that he described some of the pictures in this show as capable of being grasped at one glance, Milne considered himself a modernist. He stated that in contrast to older "browsing" pictures which were detailed, complicated, and involved travelling round and round within the rectangle, "the modernist's movement is much simpler, might be indicated by a single gesture, a wave of the hand. Coming down to more familiar ground many of the arrangements in my pictures at Mellors were as simple as this. The one of the hanging lamp and shelves, just one sweep and out."[45] Only in the quick diagrammatic analyses of these pictures in his letters did he allow himself to dispense with the object entirely.

It has been intimated that through these pictures, Milne was responding to the prevailing artistic climate which was "ripe for abstraction."[46] However, it was less a response to external stimuli than a logical step in his development; for in fact, the spark that had ignited interest in abstraction in Toronto around 1927 had been all but extinguished by 1935. Two of the main early advocates of abstraction, Lawren S. Harris (1885–1970) and Bertram Brooker, were not raising their voices in support of abstraction in Canada at that time. Harris had taken up residence in the United States in 1934, and Brooker had returned to a more representational idiom, influenced by the conservative climate of the art world between the two world wars. Milne's *Across the Still Lake*, 1936 [13], could be compared with a nearly contemporary work by Charles Comfort, *Clearing, Big Stone Bay, Lake of the Woods*, 1934. Comfort's sympathy to early abstraction in Canada in the late 1920s and early 1930s is evident in the formalized patterning of this small oil on panel. But in comparison with Milne, it shows little evidence that the artist had a deeper understanding of modernism – specifically a concern with the autonomous nature of art. Milne would probably have felt that Comfort's reliance on outside sources robbed the work of the essential element of "creative courage," as he felt it did with L.L. FitzGerald.

In Milne's casting of darts and laurels, Bertram Brooker was the ultimate loser, and A.Y. Jackson and J.W. Morrice (1865–1924) the all-time winners. On the basis of fifteen works by Jackson he saw in the Group of Seven exhibition at the Art Gallery of Toronto in the spring of 1930 (part of Milne's efforts to inform himself about Canadian art after having been out of touch for so long), Milne expressed the opinion that Jackson was the "greatest living Canadian painter." In the flowing rhythm of line which consistently pervades the entire composition, Milne saw something truly original (creative courage) – inspired by modernist influence, yet something Jackson had made his own. Milne appreciated the line for its independent qualities, not for its application to, say, the picturesque bell-cast roofs, which partook of the general pictorial rhythm as a matter of course. "It is all a river, a river of shapes and color flowing in at one side of his canvas and out at the other," he wrote of Jackson's work,[47] words which could be used to describe *Early Spring, Quebec*, 1927. Milne approached the work of others as he did his own, applying the same criteria, similarly reading their paintings in formal terms. Milne painted *The Blind Road*, 1930 [14], around the same time as he made these observations about Jackson's work. Because of the strong influence his drypoint etchings had on his painting at that time, imparting to them a strong linear quality, it is not surprising that he was particularly sensitive to the linear element in Jackson's work.

James Wilson Morrice, the expatriate Canadian, was also highly praised by Milne. After viewing a Morrice exhibition at the Art Gallery of Toronto in May 1932, Milne decided that Morrice was a pure painter. "Everything was subordinated to aesthetic emotion, which he gets almost entirely by color and line in the later, more successful ones, – the green Trinidads, you find little reliance on form, a few larger loosely drawn masses.... He gets great simplicity and unity." In this, Milne compared him to Monet.[48] In Milne's eyes, Morrice missed greatness by failing to inject anything personal into his art – though Milne tentatively proposed that Morrice's peculiar suppression of chromatic values (favouring rose, sky blue and jade green over red, blue and green) might consitute that personal element.

Of all his Canadian contemporaries, Milne was most critical of Bertram Brooker, for he found nothing original in his art: "A fervent appreciator – now this, now that. So thorough is his appreciation that he can reproduce his model with

Charles Comfort. **Clearing, Big Stone Bay, Lake of the Woods**. 1934. Oil on board, 26 x 30. Art Gallery of Ontario, Toronto, 85/253.

A.Y. Jackson. **Early Spring, Quebec**, 1927. Oil on canvas, 53 x 66. Art Gallery of Ontario, Toronto, 135.

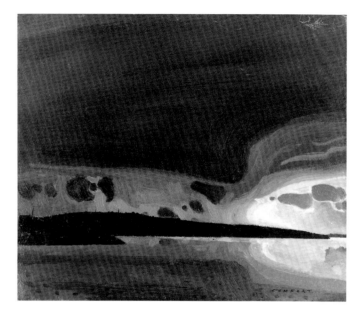

13 ACROSS THE STILL LAKE. 1936. Oil on canvas, 31.3 x 36.6. Art Gallery of Ontario, Toronto, 86/91.

14 BLIND ROAD. 1930. Oil on canvas, 40.6 x 51. Private collection.

complete understanding...."[49] The two works Brooker showed in the 1930 Group of Seven show, *Snow Fugue* and *Landscape*, Milne saw as completely derivative of Lawren S. Harris. Milne had no respect for copyists. He was acutely aware of the grip that Cézanne's influence was having on his contemporaries, and highly critical of their succumbing to this influence. Having admired Cézanne and Matisse himself in his formative years, Milne had successfully integrated their influence into his work. He observed that the American Leon Kroll, whose work he saw exhibited in Toronto, "... looked at Cézanne and said... there's something there, if that were worked out more completely it would be good. He has worked it out, applied, adapted, finished, enlarged, combined – and lost it. He has nothing but a mixture, hash, very imposing but without the thrill."[50] The most serious flaw he found in Clive Bell's argument was the critic's complete absorption with Cézanne to the point of being blinded to the merits of any artist who chose a different path.

The reason for Milne's harsh criticism of Brooker's art is probably that the work failed to meet his high expectations. Milne had been deeply impressed by a talk that Brooker delivered on El Greco at the Art Gallery of Toronto on 28 March 1930, part of a series of "Illustrated Lectures on Great Artists." He referred to it as "thrilling," and noted that: "The high spot of the winter for me, was not an exhibition but a lecture on El Greco by a man named Brooker."[51] It later prompted Milne to refer to him as "my magnificent Brooker!" It was probably less the images themselves, and more Brooker's insightful comments on El Greco's work that elicited such praise from Milne, who was well versed in art criticism himself, as his letters indicate.

It seems highly plausible that Milne personally identified with the subject of the talk as presented by Brooker. For example, Brooker revealed that "El Greco's indifference to the public opinion of his day, his courage in the face of much opposition and his determination to pursue his own individuality... brings him close to the people of today...," and that rather than being the product of one school of painting or one school of thought, "he has taken something from the best of several schools, which he has woven with his own personality to produce something unique...."[52] Could this not also describe the work of David Milne?

There are various aspects of his artistic expression and philosophy that Milne shared with his contemporaries, for he was a product of his age and synthesized many diverse influences of that age into his painting. Because he was never a follower, and never established a school (his form of expression being perhaps too personal), Milne's work continues to avoid categorization. His criticisms of the art of his contemporaries, running parallel to his unrelenting self-criticism, do, however, offer some idea of where Milne "fits" in relation to others of his generation.

Milne may be studied from many points of view, for his art bridges the nineteenth and twentieth centuries, reaches across national boundaries, and links nature and artifice (naturalism and abstraction). In this, he is perhaps closest to J.W. Morrice, with whom he overlapped in time, but Milne is more fully of this continent and of this century. His art is an extremely refined distillation of the visual world seen through early twentieth-century eyes, and will continue to be valued as one of the most original contributions to twentieth-century art in North America.

15 9TH AVENUE EL. New York, c. 1910–12. Charcoal on paper, 42.5 x 48.
Private collection.

David Milne's New York

Lora Senechal Carney

■ "The McFee book is out and it is one fine job," Milne's friend James Clarke wrote to him in 1918; "… he has gotten an amazing lot out of the most commonplace events of New Jersey and a very fine slant on New York itself."[1]

William McFee's novel *Aliens* was a comment on America by a writer and ship's engineer who landed in New York City in 1912 after a thirty-year life spent mostly at sea. Its "slant on New York" develops through striking passages such as the following, in which the book's narrator looks up toward Manhattan from a ship docked at Staten Island:

In the middle distance stood the statue of Liberty, islanded in the incoming tide-way, while away beyond, rising in superb splendour from a pearly haze, the innumerable towers of Manhattan floated and gleamed before my eyes. Irresistibly there came to me a memory of Turner's Venetian masterpieces, and I knew that even that great magician would have seized upon the scene before me with avidity, would have delighted in the fairy-like threads of the bridges, the poetic groupings of the vast buildings, and the innumerable fenestrations of the campanili.… Here the Queen of the Adriatic was indeed resuscitated and the Venetian Republic born to a sublimer destiny. Surely the same indomitable spirit, the same high courage, that had reared that wondrous city out of the sea, was here before me, piling story upon story, pinnacle beyond pinnacle, till our old-world hearts sickened and our unaccustomed brains grew dizzy at the sight.[2]

New York City was an early-twentieth-century phenomenon, and William McFee's sublime description was one of the countless thousands of images it inspired – written, photographed, drawn and painted from every imaginable physical and cultural viewpoint.

In the year McFee wrote *Aliens*, David Milne produced his first major group of New York City subjects. Unlike McFee, Milne was not a newcomer to the context they briefly shared; Milne had been in the city since 1903 and had made the beginnings of a painting reputation there. He and his partner Amos Engle[3] had established a business address on East Forty-Second Street, where they made "showcards," hand-lettered (and sometimes illustrated) display cards for store windows and counters. Milne also worked for illustrated magazines, although we do not yet know the extent of that activity. He had close friendships in New York, and in 1912 married a New Yorker, May ("Patsy") Hegarty from Brooklyn.

His painting was maturing; in fact, his Manhattan pictures are his first independent series. They reveal that from a formal point of view, he was now closely in sympathy with those European modernist painters who rejected illusionistic space and form in favour of expressive contour, brushstroke and colour: the impressionists, Bonnard, Whistler, the Fauves.[4] Although Milne was not involved in the famous avant-garde circles of Alfred Stieglitz and of Louise and Walter Arensburg, his urban pictures situate him within the first generation of American modernists, a generation which is generally considered to have reached early maturity around 1910.[5]

Was it a coincidence that city scenes replaced his landscapes just as he emerged with a coherent modernist style? A look at the overall New York artistic scene before World War I suggests that it probably was not. John Marin's coming-out work, for instance, also involved a heavy emphasis on Manhattan subjects, and other members of the Stieglitz circle similarly chose to paint the city as a sign of their own modernity. Even earlier, Robert Henri and the "Ashcan School" of painters, while not formally innovative, had made the painting of New York streets and city life the basis of a major rebellion against outworn academy tradition. Maurice Prendergast, who exhibited with Henri's group but who worked in a post-impressionist style, also painted New York scenes.

However, the simple fact of choosing to make a New York City image is far less interesting and important than *what* one includes when one paints (or writes, photographs or draws) such an image. Milne's New York pictures have been studied in recent scholarship mostly for their formal qualities, because they marked his entry into modernism. I would like to consider these images for their urban content and juxtapose them with those of McFee, Marin and others, in an effort to discover what Milne's vision of the city, once defined, can reveal about him as a painter.

LORA S. CARNEY

New York City as the young artists of Milne's generation knew it was constantly measuring itself against the rest of the world and coming out on top; an unabashed boosterism issued from the place. It had annexed Brooklyn, the Bronx, Staten Island and Queens in 1898, just as the recession of the 1890s was ending, and was now gaining population at a stunning speed. New York City was the world's largest port. It had the world's biggest bridges: in fact, "To say that they are the greatest bridges in the world is but a small statement, for nowhere else in the world are there bridges even to be compared with them."[6] The world's "largest and most costly hotel" was the Plaza on Central Park South, just completed in 1907.[7] A 1908–9 text titled "New York – The World's Commercial Centre" stated, for example, that 19,739 apartment houses had been built in the city in the previous six years, and that it now also hosted two thousand publishing and printing houses and a hundred playhouses.[8]

This was "the New New York" which replaced the centuries-old, quiet port city, leaving hardly a trace. It was the ultimate example of modern industrial "progress," and it displayed what must have been at least to some a horrifying disregard for what was lost. "Never was there any other city that so rapidly and ruthlessly tears down and throws away…. Nothing, however new and costly, is permitted to stand for a moment in the path of public or private improvement. For new thoroughfares, for burrowing subways, for bridge approaches, massed houses vanish; and other buildings, in number innumerable, vanish that there may arise triumphant business structures or apartment houses such as elsewhere the world has never seen."[9]

Photography, especially commercial photography, was an essential tool of New York's boosterism. Peter B. Hale, in *Silver Cities: The Photography of American Urbanization, 1839–1915*, states that photography in America had had a long-standing propagandistic role in the cities: it "advertised and celebrated change – most fundamentally the transformation of America from a rural and agrarian nation to an urban and industrial one."[10] In several early-twentieth-century New York publications, notably *King's Views of New York*, this role is clearly being played out, and the rising Manhattan skyline, with each new "world's tallest building" appearing in succession, is featured in photograph after photograph.

To William McFee, Manhattan's downtown skyscrapers in their "poetic groupings" were the *campanili* of an overpowering New World Venice. Collectively they allowed him to treat the city as a sublime image, inspiring the same awe that artists found a century previous in the world's great mountains and waterfalls.

Skyscrapers were the ultimate symbols of the city, and it is natural that these "triumphant business structures" would also appear in painted images of modern New York. "Skyscraperism" in fact became a notable phenomenon among visual artists.[11] John Marin, on a trip back to New York from Europe in early 1910, painted views of lower Manhattan streets and of the skyline seen from the Brooklyn Bridge, in which the great heights as well as the familiar shapes of the most famous office towers are emphasized.[12] He continued to paint such views upon returning from Europe the following year, and he produced futurist-like Manhattan pictures in 1913 which represent the dynamism of the city through the tilting of planes and lines ("I see great forces at work – great movements; the large buildings and the small buildings; the warring of the great and the small …").[13] Marin's contemporary Max Weber produced New York paintings from 1912 to 1915, most of them highly abstracted and based on synthetic cubism. In a still-representational example from 1912, however, based on a photograph taken from the top of the Singer Building by his friend Alvin Langdon Coburn, Weber gives a dramatic perspective down toward a second skyscraper, the Liberty Tower.[14] Abraham Walkowitz, another Stieglitz Circle artist, produced abstracted skyscraper images which he called "Improvisations of New York," using, as William Innes Homer states, "various means of transforming the city into a visually dynamic image, working not from nature but rather letting his imagination run free."[15]

In spite of all that Milne had in common with these artists, he did not involve himself in "skyscraperism."[16] The dynamic, "progressive" view of New York which others seemed to equate with cutting-edge modernism, and which paralleled so closely the attitude of the city fathers, was not Milne's view. He generally painted only low and medium-sized buildings, and when he did include skyscrapers, as in *Waterfront*, 1911 or 1912 [**22**], his treatment of them indicates a lack of enthusi-

asm. This composition has layers of progressively higher buildings behind low ones; the overlapping creates the picture's space. Since the picture as a whole is defined in only the broadest terms, the buildings are not easily identifiable. In fact we can conclude this is a view of lower Manhattan only by comparing it with a closely related Milne watercolour titled *Battery Park* (c. 1913, MFC). However, the vaguest of all the buildings in *Waterfront* are the two skyscrapers. Not only are they relatively pale and flat, but their contours have been obscured by smoke. They have less presence and power than the undistinguished buildings in front of them.

We find a similar effect in paintings made by the leading American impressionist Childe Hassam around the turn of the century. Hassam was one of the first to introduce skyscrapers into paintings, but in *Late Afternoon, Winter, New York*, 1900, for example, he barely distinguishes the lone skyscraper in the background from the sky surrounding it. Art historian Donelson Hoopes suggests that Hassam "offers veils of poetic atmosphere to soften the harsh outlines of the giant building in the distance and so returns this changing world to a more gentle time."[17] A 1905 reviewer saw in another of Hassam's pictures the same intent: "a poetic presentment of a scene with which possibly few would associate poesy, namely the New York Hudson River front, with the skyscrapers in evidence to be sure, but softened by a shimmering hazy atmosphere."[18] Milne's *Waterfront* is not nostalgic, and he was not attempting to poeticize a prose subject, but certainly he did not celebrate it any more than Hassam did.

On the other hand, Milne also avoided negative emotional extremes; for instance, the horror William McFee expressed in this passage from the novel *Casuals of the Sea*, where the young British sailor, Hannibal, views New York from the Battery:

The roar of it, and the immensity of it, appalled him.... Hannibal's gaze returned again and again to the tremendous buildings with their innumerable windows, tier on tier to the sky, their giant towers and stark outlines. It seemed to him that there was a personal antagonism in this monstrous conglomeration of alien energy, and he felt afraid. What would they think of it at home?... And yet as his eyes took in the more immediate details, he saw old men and slatternly women on the seats around them dozing in the heat, very like people on seats at home.[19]

Another characteristic of Milne's Manhattan paintings is his avoidance of views up or down the narrow, steep-walled downtown streets which have so often been compared to canyons. In *Waterfront* as well as in his "billboard" street scenes, Milne chose for himself frontal or very modestly diagonal positions relative to the buildings. This habit places him in striking contrast to John Marin, and even more to Joseph Pennell, who made illustrations for books and for articles in major New York magazines such as *The Century* and *Harper's*.[20] Pennell was primarily an etcher and lithographer after the manner of Whistler, and his work, like Whistler's, was shown frequently in New York and admired by Milne.[21] Pennell's subjects were views of European and American cities which focussed on what he regarded as each city's characteristic architecture. He did various series of New York City etchings. The first, from 1904, has several views into lower Manhattan streets, and one is actually titled *Canyon, No. 1*.[22] Strengthening the impression of chasms in these etchings are the human figures thronging the streets, made absolutely tiny.

Pennell's second series, from 1908, includes *The Unbelievable City*, showing lower Manhattan

LORA S. CARNEY

from the south as Milne's *Waterfront* does. Pennell's vision of the city, however, includes an expansive setting: the river and a glorifying sky surround the buildings. By contrast, Milne's waterfront seems a grey, closed-off fragment. Moreover, Pennell's view is split by Broadway, and the exaggerated vertical of the predominant Singer Building emphasizes that division. "It is marvellous, incredible," Pennell wrote later. "When you go out on the ferry to Staten Island, there is one moment on the trip when, looking back to Manhattan, you see the city cleft by the canyon of Broadway. I say that the Grand Canyon has nothing to equal that sight. If Broadway were a street in a European city, centuries old, Americans would flock there to visit it."[23]

Pennell loved the whole optimistic notion of human progress through technological advance and work: "While in other days popes and princes built churches and palaces which are still the wonder of the world, today Commerce and Industry are doing work equally impressive.... The mills and docks and canals and bridges of the present are more mighty, more pictorial, and more practical than any similar works of the past; they are the true temples of the present."[24] New York epitomized that notion and he loved it accordingly, expressing his feeling just as the urban enthusiast John Marin did, by embracing the most extreme manifestations of its urban character. Milne was not inclined this way.

Milne's 1912 street scenes with billboards were in the mainstream of his New York City production, and *Billboards* [26], *Columbus Monument* [27] and *White Matrix* [28] are typical works from that brief period. Some were made in midtown Manhattan where he and Amos Engle had their showcard shop, just off Fifth Avenue on East Forty-Second Street. The streets in this area still had a more human scale than those downtown. It was not quiet though: Benjamin Altman's had moved to a large store at Fifth Avenue and Thirty-Fifth Street in 1906, and other major retailers soon followed them up the Avenue. Thus the area rapidly changed from a residential to a fashionable shopping district. "It will contain nothing but hotels and shops – the most expensive in the city; and it will constitute the center of the distinctively metropolitan life of the metropolis...."[25] Another dramatic change to the Avenue at midtown which contributed to its increasingly public character, was the building of the New York Public Library [24] during the first decade of the century, just around the corner from Milne and Engle's shop. (The library, with its Fifth Avenue facade modelled after the east front of the Louvre, was such a large and important symbol of the progress of American culture that President Taft was there to help open it in May 1911.)

Beyond the specifics of that area, which was after all only one of his painting locations, Milne's street pictures reflect a change that had overtaken the whole city, as well as other great cities, before the turn of the century: as urban cores became denser and living spaces became smaller, people were spending more time in public. They were on the streets and sidewalks at all times of the day. "Now the *flaneur* seems at last to have made his appearance. New York ... is at last taking on definite resemblance to that aspect of 'all the world' in virtue of which it is 'a stage'."[26]

The street activity, the library, the new gas-powered double-decker Fifth Avenue buses, are all there in Milne's bright, sunlit street scenes of 1912. The billboard paintings happen to be rather like "a stage" in the way figures are ranged against a space made shallow by a backdrop of billboards and shop walls. However, that analogy

Childe Hassam. **Late Afternoon, New York**. 1900. Oil on canvas, 94 x 74. Brooklyn Museum, New York, 62.68.

Joseph Pennell. **The Unbelievable City**. 1908. Etching, 21 x 28. Picker Art Gallery, Colgate University, Hamilton, NY, 1977.21.

16 WICKER CHAIR.
New York, 1914.
Oil on canvas, 50.8 x 45.8.
Agnes Etherington Art
Centre, bequest of
Mrs J.P. Barwick, 28-8.

does not extend beyond the superficial. Milne did not paint street life as theatre, and this becomes especially obvious when one compares his pictures to such images as John Sloan's *New York City Life*, a set of ten etchings made 1905–06. Sloan's titles alone – *Man Monkey*, *Fifth Avenue Critics*, *Fun*, *One Cent* – show why this Ashcan School artist is often said to have made the human comedy the central subject of his work.[27] What seems to characterize Milne's street paintings, from the point of view of urban content, is, by contrast, a sense of detachment.

Clearly Milne's modernist alignment would have prevented him from employing the strongly narrative elements which characterized Sloan's pictures. However, Maurice Prendergast, the modernist to whose paintings Milne's billboard scenes have always been compared most closely, showed substantially more engagement with his figures than Milne.

In Prendergast's city pictures, figures hold a child's hand, hold dogs' leashes, hold onto their hats, converse. Prendergast's figures relax; they are often pursuing some leisure activity.[28] Nancy Mowll Mathews, in the catalogue for the 1990 Whitney Museum Prendergast retrospective, states that in fact Prendergast had a genuine sympathy with the "common people," and that his expression of this, especially in his New York City paintings, puts him closer to the populist viewpoint of the Ashcan School than is usually thought.[29]

Milne's 1912 figures, relative to Prendergast's, are stiff; we read them first of all as sets of fashionable contours. Compared to Milne's own figures in interiors of a couple of years later (*Wicker Chair* [16], *Black* [6], *Red* [5]), they are unsympathetic. We usually see them only from a reserved distance, from the other side of a street or across an open boulevard or a city square or

circle. We are led to think that although Milne had a certain amount of success in synthesizing formal elements in these pictures, street painting had not proved to be a particularly comfortable category for him, especially given the fact that he did not stay with it long.

It was in 1913, especially during and after a productive summer holiday at West Saugerties in the Catskills,[30] that Milne went seriously into landscape painting, and the city then took up less of his attention. The watercolour *Billboard*, c. 1913 [17], at the final stage of the billboard series, predicts the direction his work would now take: the natural forms, the pair of trees, have increased importance in relation to the urban forms, the billboard and now-tiny buildings to the left. The two-dimensional patterning of the picture surface thus has a more organic character than did the rectilinear billboard pictures before it, and it is a much more confident picture.

The beautiful *Botanical Museum, Bronx Park*, 1915, a watercolour of a subject Milne painted often in his last two years in the city, has the integration of building and natural forms that characterized the city pictures of this period. The forms of the trees now dominate the picture completely.

Documentation for the period of Milne's New York City images is so scarce that we have little sense of what he did from day to day; we mainly understand his life then through reminiscences he wrote decades later in Canada. As a verbal statement of his attitude to the city, we have only his laconic response of a few years previous to his future wife's desire to live in the country: "I am quite willing. In fact, I for my part prefer it very much."[31] But this response fits exactly with what we know through his paintings. The majority of his known works done before 1912 are land-

17 BILLBOARD. 1912. Watercolour over graphite on paperboard, 38 x 50.7.
Private collection.

scapes, most of them probably executed in what were then rural and semi-rural sections of upper Manhattan and the Bronx; and once he left New York City in 1916, he became, not exclusively but nevertheless in essence, a landscape painter for life. His urban paintings were an interlude for him in terms of subject matter, crucial as they were to the development of his style.

Griselda Pollock summarizes the well-known notion of late-nineteenth-century "modernity" by saying that it is urban, it "stands for a myriad of responses to the vast increase in population leading to the literature of the crowds and masses, a speeding up of the pace of life with its attendant changes in the sense and regulation of time and fostering that very modern phenomenon, fashion, the shift in the character of towns and cities … with production becoming less visible while the centres of cities … become key sites of consumption and display.…"[32] Milne, having grown up in the country, experienced "modern" life in New York City with an intensity he would not have felt anywhere else in North America. He allowed it into his paintings, but not at full force. He adopted the stylistic principles of modernism and employed them fully for the first time in his urban work, but he only reached his heights as an artist after he left the city for upstate New York.

No doubt he was aware of the parallel with the modernist whom he occasionally claimed had influenced him most, Monet. Monet was alive, famous and working at Giverny during Milne's years in the city, and first-rate Monets of all periods appeared regularly at Durand-Ruel's and elsewhere in Manhattan. Before 1908, when Alfred Stieglitz began showing avant-garde art, Monet was the most radical artist around New York. Even another French impressionist looked tame by comparison; having seen a Pissarro show in Durand-Ruel's main exhibition room, a *New York Times* reviewer commented that "the difference between his work and that of … Monet is seen when one leaves the gallery and catches sight of one of Monet's brilliant canvases in the outer rooms. Then one realizes how difficult it is for the disciple to emulate the master, whose creative force is seen in all that he touches.…"[33] Milne had before him the high-profile example of a painter who, having experienced the modern city and developed an approach to painting while there, could then leave and continue to grow in stature as an artist for the rest of his life. Milne would do this too. Like Monet, he would go on to paint a natural world made all the more precious and rare by his experience of the modern city.

18 CHESTNUT AND LAUREL. West Saugerties, 1914. Oil on canvas, 61 x 51.1.
Private collection.

19 JEROME AVENUE, THE BRONX. New York, probably 1915. Watercolour and ink over pencil on paper, 42 x 50.8. National Gallery of Canada, Ottawa, 6375.

20 GRAY, BROWN AND BLACK. New York, 1915. Oil on canvas, 61.3 x 66.1. National Gallery of Canada, Ottawa, 16525.

48

21 SPUYTEN DUYVIL. 1910. Pastel on wove paper, 37.2 x 46.4.
Milne Family Collection.

22 WATERFRONT.
New York,
c. 1911–12. Oil on canvas,
50.8 x 45.8. National
Gallery of Canada, Ottawa,
16551.

23 THE BLOSSOM
PICKERS.
New York, c. 1911–12.
Oil on canvas, 66.2 x 60.7.
Milne Family Collection.

24 FIFTH AVENUE FROM THE STEPS OF THE NEW YORK PUBLIC LIBRARY.
New York, c. 1911. Etching, 13.8 x 14.8. Milne Family Collection.

25 GREY BILLBOARDS.
New York, c. 1911–12.
Oil on canvas, 61 x 50.8.
Milne Family Collection.

26 BILLBOARDS. *New York, c. 1912. Oil on canvas, 51.2 x 56.5.*
National Gallery of Canada, Ottawa, 9850.

Every week-day from one o'clock on, I was at 8 (now 20) East 42nd Street making money; every morning I painted somewhere in the streets, parks or suburbs, everywhere, in front of the public library, on Columbus Circle, in Van Cortlandt and Bronx Parks, at the Erie Basin, along the Hudson, on the East River. For several years this kept up. I had a partner in both art and showcards, and our shop came to be a meeting place. When fellow students came in, the battle of art raged, while my partner and myself feverishly applied the lettering brush, at the same time never failing to keep up our side — rather our two sides -- of the aesthetic war. . . .
Massey Letter

27 COLUMBUS MONUMENT. New York, c. 1912. Oil on canvas, 50.8 x 45.7. Milne Family Collection.

David Milne employs a kind of telegraphic notation by dots and dashes of color and broken-up masses that results in dramatic force of description. His two figures in a doorway are amusingly unlike all other figures in doorways. (This subject fairly runs riot in the present exhibition.) They are quite violently alive, and send the pictures around them back into a shadowy and invalid region. Mr Prendergast's pictures have the same effect; they are like a cluster of red-cheeked hoydens bursting into a mid-Victorian assembly of anemic ladies. Possibly a trifle too noisy to live with, but certainly refreshing to encounter on a Sunday stroll.
— New York Times, 1912

28 WHITE MATRIX. New York, c. 1912. Watercolour over pencil on paper mounted on illustration board, 50.8 x 61. Milne Family Collection.

29 ALCOVE. *New York, c. 1914. Oil on canvas, 50.8 x 63.5.*
Milne Family Collection.

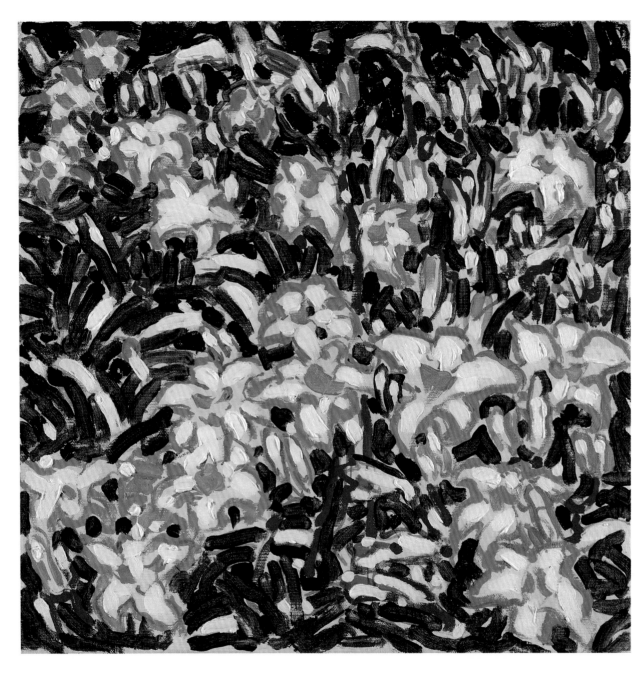

30 LILIES. Probably West Saugerties, c. 1914. Oil on canvas, 50.8 x 50.8. McMichael Canadian Art Collection, Kleinburg, Ontario, gift of the Founders, Robert and Signe McMichael, 1966.16.18.

31 WOOD INTERIOR IV. West Saugerties, 1914. Watercolour over pencil on paper, 46.1 x 44.8.
Milne Family Collection.

32 PALISADES TREES. New York, 1914. Watercolour over pencil on paper, 58.2 x 46.1. Milne Family Collection.

33 GRAND CONCOURSE, BRONX. New York, c. 1914–15. Oil on canvas, 50.8 x 61.
Art Gallery of Ontario, Toronto, bequest of Mrs J.P. Barwick, 85/126.

Painting was started quickly but for a long time was not good. There was no difficulty getting used to new subjects, the trouble was that my painting, before I left New York, had taken an unfortunate turn, maybe reflecting a troubled frame of mind. The pictures were mannered, heavy, spotty and lacking any sensitiveness or subtlety. Very few were of any interest. The colour was mostly green, black and white and in some of the buildings a reddish brown. . . . I don't remember how long it took for the ease and steadiness of life at Boston Corners to have a noticeable effect on painting. A few months, perhaps. It was a good painting place because it was a good place for a painter to live, demands on him were fewer than in any other place I knew. . . .
Autobiography, 1947
[MFP]

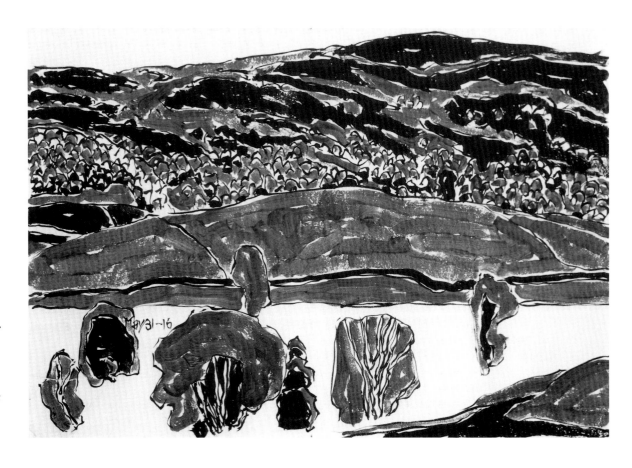

34 JOE LEE'S HILL (GREEN MASSES). Boston Corners, 31 May 1916. Watercolour over pencil on paper, 38.5 x 56.3. National Gallery of Canada, Ottawa, 16522.

I have very little interest in art as a technical performance, an accomplishment, a superficial matter of the trained eye and hand. I think of it, rather, as a way of life, shaped and moulded by influences before the artist's birth, by his training, particularly in the very early years, and by every event and circumstance of his life.[1]

■ In May of 1916 David Milne left New York and settled in the village of Boston Corners. His departure was precipitated by a variety of factors — economic, emotional and aesthetic. Milne had never been happy dividing himself between what he distinguished as "painting and illustrating"[2] and, despite some success with exhibiting, found that

keeping an apartment, painting in the morning, doing showcards in the afternoon and sending pictures to fruitless exhibitions was rather too much for one human being.[3]

Milne's emotional and physical discomfort led to nervous exhaustion and he spent the summer of 1914 in the country, at West Saugerties, recovering his health. The situation did not improve upon his return to the city. The following year saw both a personal and an aesthetic crisis.

Although Milne was later to describe this "final break with the city" as "a tragedy,"[4] it was crucial to his development as an artist. While the opportunities to exhibit were severely reduced and Milne did not often get to devote himself full-time to painting, by leaving the fractured life of New York he was able to focus both his life and art. The work carried out just prior to his leaving New York is some of the blackest of his career. The formal problems of paintings such as *Grey, Brown and Black* [20] did not permit easy solutions and the use of simple massed shapes, as in *Large Tree* [9] and *Botanical Museum, Bronx Park*, 1915,

did not offer a way out. The change afforded by the move to Boston Corners was gradual but critical and helped Milne to re-establish his formal direction.

Boston Corners was not a chance discovery. It was like finding a star or element. Certain facts about it were known beforehand, or at least required. It had to be within reasonable train distance of New York, yet beyond commuting range and it had to be suitable for painting, preferably with some hills to sit on while painting other hills. If there were interesting things between the hills, such as a village or lakes or ponds, so much the better.[5]

Milne apparently thought about this move for some time and, with his friend James Clarke, took the trouble to study topographical maps to determine a likely location. They decided on Boston Corners, a small hamlet in rural New York State, and set out to explore it one weekend in the spring of 1916. An extensive walking survey, Milne's fondness for the area, and the availability of a house resulted in a decision to move.

The fact that the Milnes soon "settled in the house under the mountain"[6] suggests that he was ready for a change. Painting began almost immediately and Milne had "no difficulty getting used to new subjects."[7] *Joe Lee's Hill* [34] retains the strong linear qualities of the 1915 ink drawings while reasserting Milne's interest in colour.

In his unpublished Boston Corners Autobiography, Milne described the work of this period as "mannered, heavy, spotty and lacking any sensitiveness or subtlety."[8] The evidence suggests that it did take Milne some time to determine his direction. His interests were diverse — strong linear patterns, colour, texture and, increasingly, light. It took some time to integrate all of these concerns; nevertheless, Milne was too harsh in his assessment of the work.

Boston Corners
Ian M. Thom

The Boulder [**44**] is indeed "spotty" but lacks in neither "sensitiveness or subtlety." The means are kept to a minimum but the control of colour, line and texture keep an extremely complex image legible. The interest in the flow of light recalls images such as *Palisades Trees* [**32**] and *Chestnut and Laurel* [**18**] but also suggests other directions for exploration. The range of colours in *The Boulder* is limited, but continues Milne's use of colour for aesthetic rather than veristic purposes. The interest in pattern recalls the concerns of the post-impressionist artists whose work Milne had seen in New York. *Relaxation* [**45**] is one of a number of works which use colour in an arbitrary manner but which successfully tread the line between purely abstract pattern and a sentimental depiction of a pleasant outdoor scene. The use of the white of the paper to unify the whole, and the integration of line and distinct patches of colour suggest that Milne had gone beyond the starkness of the 1915–16 ink drawings.

Boston Corners meant new subjects and Milne spent a good deal of time exploring the area around the village. Bishop's Pond and the Kelly Ore Bed, a short distance away, provided him with what was to become one of his most important subjects – reflections. The watercolour of 4 October 1916 [**46**] is one of the most successful of these early Boston Corners images. It was not, however, easily achieved. A close examination of the work reveals that a section on the left has been pasted onto the main sheet, suggesting that Milne thought better of some element of the composition. This does not detract from the ultimate success of the image.

Over a loose framework of graphite lines, Milne has used an extremely restricted range of colour. The image is divided into three distinct sections – the foreground (the shore of the pond), the pond itself and the far shore. The foreground introduces a diagonal which leads into the composition and acts to force our attention on the pond. In contrast to the austere, dry paint surface of the shores, the pond's rich liquidity brilliantly suggests the shift in texture between land and water. Milne has deliberately made this shift as startling as possible, but with simple means. The shore is elaborated just enough to be easily read. The reflections were first painted as dryly as the shore, but Milne went over them with a wash, and the lines bled to give this part of the image a soft focus.

Milne was not however satisfied with the "gray woolen patch"[9] which the bleeding of the black lines created, and worked towards eliminating all but the most subtle change in texture. "The adventure in these pool pictures was one of texture, of contrast between the harsh, clear cut colour and line of trees and contours, and the intimate combination of the two in the reflections."[10]

Milne had for some years felt very confident using black, and to this base added more and more colour in 1917. *Black Reflections (Reflected Forms)* [**48**][11] is notable for the introduction of a brilliant red which animates the whole composition. Milne had not articulated his theory of controlling the movement of the viewer's eye at this point in his career, but we can clearly see his attempt to direct our eye across the surface. The washed-over area of black is a foil to the row of silhouetted trees.

Keen observation of the landscape informed all Milne's works of the period, but he used artistic sources as well. *Trees in Spring* [**47**] is related, as John O'Brian has suggested, to the patterns of an ancient Egyptian relief.[12] The flat forms and linear skeletons of the trees reflect Milne's formal interests. The image is less concerned with texture than some of the watercolours of the period but develops a complex space more successfully than

IAN M. THOM

64

the earlier New York City landscapes. This is achieved, in part, by the use of the whites to show the light touching the tops of the trees. These bright patches break up the expanse of green and act as a group of "dazzle" spots to excite and direct the eye.[13]

Milne continued to experiment with textures throughout 1917. In *Sunburst over the Catskills* [36] "the texture change was between distant mountains and clouds and the foreground."[14]

The Boston Corners landscape had become a rich source of subject matter for Milne and his approach to it is recorded in an exceptional passage in the autobiography.

Painting subjects were scattered all over the place but rarely were more than two miles away. All were painted on the spot, and then, good or bad, left alone: no attempt was made to develop or change or repaint after the original painting was done. I had to carry a wooden paint box, easel, stretched watercolour paper or canvas and, when I went to the limits of my painting territory, my lunch, cold tea or coffee in a jar, sandwiches, cake if it was to be had, even pie, when there was pie. The radius of my painting ground was determined by time, load and frame of mind. If my attention hadn't escaped from the round of day by day events and become fixed on painting subjects and painting methods within the leisurely two mile walk it wasn't apt to that day. The pattern of these day long painting trips was always pretty much the same. The start, under full equipment, my mind occupied with my own day to day affairs with room for nothing else in it. Then the gradual shedding of this burden, leaving the vacuum to be filled with a stream of observation, first about the ways of nature as I went along, later with thoughts of painting. The Kelly Ore Bed, and its environs, two miles away, provided many painting subjects, and this day-long painting trip would be typical. The morning start, with my load, through the fence along the garden into Bishop's field, numbed by routine, with little interest in my surroundings. Then the gradual quickening, sometimes slow, sometimes fast. At first only the half conscious feel of the crispness of the grass with white frost on it. The familiar harsh scream of a blue jay or the chatter of a red squirrel might stir a comfortable familiar feeling. A minute's pause to look at a garter snake stretched beside a rock to get the first warmth of the sun. On through the scattered maples in Bishop's pasture and to the top of a rise overlooking the valley. My load would be set down while I watched and listened to the morning train coming up from New York, a long trail of smoke and steam lying on the still air. This would be a possible painting place and subject. I had seen it many times and nothing had come of it, now my mind was too sluggish to grasp anything of enough interest to start me painting. The quickening process under way but still only partly. Up with the load and on my way, observing with a little more interest tree shapes and contours. At the side of Bishop's mill pond, another halt to look at the reflections in it, feeling some excitement stirred by the colour of the trees on the opposite bank. Maples in scarlet and yellow, poplars in orange tinged with a little vermilion, the deep purple and green of ash. Some speculation about how nearly perfect the reflections in the still water are. A slight breeze springs up and the shapes in the water become less definite. A little more and they are changed to vertical waverings. Then the breeze increases and all are lost. This is not the place today. This pond with the low banks is too much exposed for my purpose. On again through Bishop's farm and across the next and the next. My thoughts now pretty much occupied with painting. The escape, the feeling of ease and well being almost complete. There is more of purpose now, of search, as I make my way across creeks, along fences, through patches of bush and up and down hills. These reflections have had some attention recently, I know what to do about them, or at least what I want to try and am busy with plans, based on what I have recently done, but with modifications based on past failures. I come to the Kelly Ore Bed, a man made pond about the size of Bishop's mill pond but with

35 THE MOUNTAINS. Near Tivoli, New York, 7 September 1917. Watercolour over pencil on paper, 39.4 x 55.9. National Gallery of Canada, Ottawa, 3019.

steep banks round two sides and a small bush at the other. Not a thing remains to remind one that it was ever anything but a quiet pool with grassy banks. Only a high wind will break its surface. This is the place. I unpack and set up my painting outfit. Quiet, leisurely, observant. I have no interest beyond what is in front of me, and what I am about to do with it.

I put a few pencil marks on paper "placing" what I want to include in the picture, moving it up and down or to either side, thinking not so much of what is there as about what I am to do with it. Then I start to draw in pencil, slowly, holding back rather than pressing on. Everything that is to go in the picture is marked in some way. The drawing is not to be followed closely, it is a sort of short hand reminder made at leisure, to be used later when work is speeded up and there isn't time to travel back and forward from the scene to paper. What happens on the paper is not so important as what goes on in my mind. By the time the drawing is finished most of the painting problems of the picture are solved, even the colour and treatment determined. I get a tin of water from the pool, fix it on the easel and set to work with colour. I work easily, rapidly now, the pool and its banks and the bush are gone, everything is on that rectangle of paper. The brush wanders over it, sometimes in great detail, sometimes broadly. I see not only what I have put down at the moment, but back to the solutions indicated in pencil and forward to what is still to be done. The pace quickens; on some rare days the painter can do no wrong (according to his own limited lights) things click into place without conscious effort, problems solve themselves, the picture seems to move under its own power. Those days are infrequent. More often there is a break in the flow somewhere along the line. Some problems may have been overlooked in the process of pencil drawing, or imperfectly solved, or shirked. Now there is a pause to consider it, an effort to grasp it. If the effort is not quickly successful the thing fades away, power is lost like escaping steam, and another failure is added to the list. When it comes to putting on paint, speed, and with it, quickening, seems to be essential. An extreme concentration, a singleness of mind. The painter must come to life, must be quickened beyond his own normal possibilities – and that is the object of the walk and of all the preparations up to the hour or so of actual painting.[15]

The direct approach to subject matter tempered by a considered editing of the motif is reflected in the most important canvas of the period – Boston Corners [50]. The composition is essentially three major bands moving up the canvas and back into space. The foreground is a screen of alternating light and dark trees which introduces the viewer to the valley which the village occupies. The buildings, Milne's "string of coloured beads,"[16] give the composition animation and colour. The image is busy but incident is kept balanced. The upper band of the hill, which would have been oppressive as a monolithic block, is broken up into areas of light and dark, greater and lesser texture.

Here Milne sits on his hill looking at another hill and there is much between to paint. This view and variations on it are amongst the most satisfying images of the period. They undoubtedly reflect Milne's satisfaction with his situation in the world and the successful resolution of the troubling formal problems which had marked the last paintings done in New York City.

The final textural innovation of Boston Corners is seen in Hillside, Berkshires [49]. The "shirting" motif is achieved by the striping of the paint: the paint ground is allowed to show between strips of paint. The effect is to give animation to the hillside while at the same time suggesting the different areas of the hill – forest, field etc. A device of remarkable subtlety, it was to be revisited after the war.

Until 1917–18, the war had little effect on Milne. He followed it with interest and concern

Our visits were mostly to Patsy's people . . . to their summer place on the Hudson, near Tivoli. . . . There was a gardener or farmer, a chicken man and a chauffeur. A little over our heads, very far away from the Boston Corners way of living, but we enjoyed it, the garden most of all. There were so many unusual fruits and vegetables and flowers. Better even than the garden for me was the painting. This was done mostly in a summer house above the river. Below me as I painted, trains were constantly rushing by, on the main line of the N.Y. Central, scooping up water just at that point from the long pans between the tracks. Then the wide river, and just across the entrance to Saugerties harbour, Saugerties village and the foothills. . . . Ten miles away the Catskills, rising abruptly, above them the clouds.
Autobiography, 1947
[MFP]

36 SUNBURST OVER THE CATSKILLS. Near Tivoli, New York, 8 September 1917. Watercolour over pencil on paper, 38.5 x 55.3. Museum of Modern Art, New York, gift of Douglas M. Duncan, 384.61.

Have done quite a bit of painting. One or two very fair in oil. Patsy and I went down to the Kelly Ore Bed the Sunday after you were here. I painted a rather large canvas and Patsy got cold feet (literally and figuratively) before I got through.
Milne to Clarke,
8 Nov 1917 [NAC]

37 POOL AND BIRCHES. Boston Corners, 21 October 1917. Oil on canvas, 56.3 x 66.4.
Art Gallery of Windsor, Ontario, gift from the Douglas M. Duncan Collection, 70.62.

Set out with the idea of carrying on the development of the dark reflections, but when I arrived I found that the subject was not suitable. The subject suggested a slightly greenish wash over the reflections but I was afraid of losing the rather slight detail. Used a barred and cloudy sky but removed it because it was confusing. It interfered with the mass of the mine buildings and the line of the top of the bank, both of which are interesting and are the resting points for the attention. The reflected part looks luminous because of the slightness of the change from the white paper to the washed over part. Notice the flowing lines of the lower part, due to the drawing in both cases — the softness of the curves and allowing the streaks to run into each other.

Boston Corners Painting Notes 117, 27 Aug 1920 [NAC]

43 WEED IRON MINES. Weed Iron Mines, near Boston Corners, 27 August 1920. Watercolour over pencil on paper, 38.5 x 55.6. National Gallery of Canada, Ottawa, 16462.

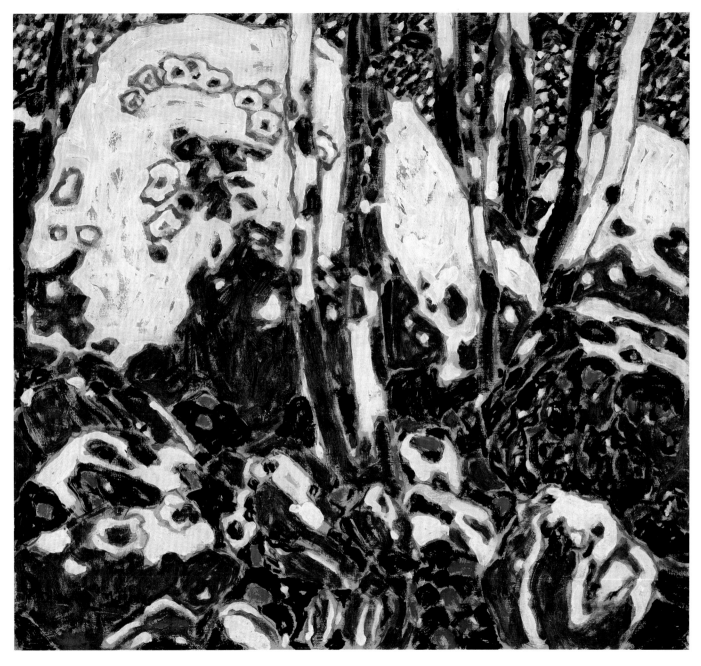

44 THE BOULDER. Boston Corners, 1916. Oil on canvas, 61.3 x 66.4. Winnipeg Art Gallery, acquired with the assistance of the Women's Committee and the Winnipeg Foundation, G62-12.

By the way if you feel like it, would you care to loan your "camouflage" one of Mrs C and Patsy at B[oston] C[orners]. I think it will be perfectly safe, though it would be away a couple of months. I think it might interest them. They have bought some pictures of camouflaged boats.
Milne to Clarke,
9 Dec 1918 [NAC]

45 RELAXATION. Boston Corners, 1916. Watercolour over pencil on paper, 38.5 x 46.7.
McMichael Canadian Art Collection, gift of the Founders, Robert and Signe McMichael, 1966.16.24.

46 BISHOP'S POND (REFLECTIONS). Boston Corners, 4 October 1916. Watercolour over pencil on paper, 44.2 x 54.3. National Gallery of Canada, Ottawa, 6380.

47 TREES IN SPRING. Boston Corners, 1917. Oil on canvas, 55.9 x 66.1.
National Gallery of Canada, Ottawa, 15387.

48 BLACK REFLECTIONS (REFLECTED FORMS). Boston Corners, 1 November 1917. Watercolour over pencil
on paper, 38.8 x 56.6. Art Gallery of Greater Victoria, BC, Women's Committee Cultural Fund, 54.17.

*Boston Corners seen from the rising ground
behind Joe Lee's Under-Mountain house was a
string of coloured beads, one end dangling into
the cut that held the two railways, one road and
one stream, and was just wide enough to hold
them. First, nearest the mountains, was the
church, small, white, with a belfry. Across the
road, a long gray house, sometimes occupied,
sometimes vacant. Beside it an old log house,
not habitable. Then Baldwin's house hidden by
orchard trees so that its colour didn't matter.
Then the red school. Next the church on the
other side was a white and yellow house, must
have been lived in by different people at different
times, I don't remember them. Beyond the school
was Joe Lee's imposing house, painted pale
green, with some other green or yellow trim, very
fine for painting. Across the road Joe Lee's barns
and silo, dark red. Beyond Joe Lee's house the
small white one where Hiram and his wife
lived. . . . Just where the road slipped down into
the cut there was another small house, gray, and
across from it on lower ground the milk station.
In the railway cut were the station and water
tank and boarding house, painted brown. Last of
all Chas. Burch's store, broad, white, with an
outside stairway. Further along was Burch's barn
and at least one other house, practically out of
town, and out of sight from my painting place
behind our house. In fact the railway buildings
and Burch's store didn't appear in the
panoramic picture. . . .*
Autobiography, 1947 [MFP]

49 HILLSIDE, BERKSHIRES. Boston Corners c. January 1918. Oil on canvas, mounted on masonite, 46.7 x 62.2. Agnes Etherington Art Centre, Queens University, Kingston, Ontario, Richardson Fund Purchase, 7-6.

50 BOSTON CORNERS. Boston Corners, 1917. Oil on canvas, 51.5 x 67.
National Gallery of Canada, Ottawa, 4603.

Nice place, Ripon, with a lot of history compressed into a small space. The camps were just outside town, half encircling it, rows of wooden huts, sometimes enclosing houses and hamlets, which were mostly occupied by Canadians. . . . Painting was improving, developing more successfully within itself. Still panoramic but less map-like and with greater use of colour. In the evenings and on holidays the town was thronged with soldiers. I was allowed to paint from a house at the head of the Skellsgate, packing small soldiers against small soldiers in the narrow way between the houses. Afterwards I was invited for Sunday dinner by the family at this house. . . .
Autobiography, 1947 [MFP]

I have been out on the Broadway, High Street, Strand of Bramshott Camp, in other words the hundred yards or so of the London-Portsmouth road that runs through tintown — an unassuming place but for all that the centre of camp life. Most of the time I was leaning against the "Soldiers Rest" trying to decide such problems as the following — what constitutes a complete back view of a man's head besides two big ears and the top of a cap? (about all I could add was a trail of cigarette smoke and a stream of bad words) — what is there in a kilt that gives even an Indian Scotchman a gait that has more action than that of any two ordinarily clad men? What makes the soles of a man's feet so prominent when he walks toward you? (The shadow and the generous proportions of the army boot, I suppose.) Etc. Etc. By the way the "Soldiers Rest" is not the name of a crooked booze emporium. It is one of the Salvation Army Huts.
Milne to Clarke, 24 March 1919 [NAC]

51 RIPON HIGH STREET. Ripon, Yorkshire, 27 February 1919. Watercolour over pencil on paper, 50.8 x 35.6. Art Gallery of Ontario, Toronto, bequest of Mrs J.P. Barwick, 85/127.

52 THE CATHOLIC WOMEN'S LEAGUE HUT, BRAMSHOTT CAMP. Bramshott, England, 14 April 1919.
Watercolour over pencil on paper, 35.6 x 50.8. National Gallery of Canada, Ottawa, 8543.

53 THE CATHEDRAL, ARRAS.
Arras, France, 30 July 1919. Watercolour over pencil on paper, two sheets, each 35.3 x 50.4. National Gallery of Canada, Ottawa, 8507, 8508.

In the winter of 1920, after I got back to Boston Corners from the War Records job, I did a good many winter pictures, some in the open, but most from a painting house I built in Joe Lee's field above the house, where I could see the house, a row of trees to the right of it, and, beyond, the mass of Fox Hill. The painting house was a success. Made out of old boards, it was just big enough for me to crawl into, and to hold me and my equipment when I was sitting down. At first I had a window in it, and, I think, a small fire in a tin can. This didn't work, the window fogged up. After that I had no fire and left the front open. The house just kept the wind off.
Autobiography, 1947
[MFP]

54 TRACK IN THE FIELDS. Boston Corners, 21 December 1919. Oil on canvas, mounted on masonite, 44.8 x 46.7. Milne Family Collection.

9:30–12:00. Gentle snowfall. Plan: To keep all very light, trees in village not veined but single masses, or outlined and with darker cores where branching is thickest, to make lower part most prominent. . . . Carried out as planned. Note drawing throughout; series of grays used, tree at right black and white, large tree black made of new blue and yellow ochre, next same with white, on houses a little permanent violet, cerulean and white.
Boston Corners Painting Notes 15, 30 Dec 1919 [NAC]

55 GENTLE SNOWFALL. Boston Corners, 30 December 1919. Oil on canvas, 45.8 x 56.3. National Gallery of Canada, Ottawa, 16552.

Planned to do this subject in oil for some time. . . . The points to be noticed are: the use of but one tone throughout; the scratchy treatment due to a desire to put the shapes on the canvas with the slightest possible means; the variety in the tree shapes secured, in some cases simply by the drawing, in others by changing the color — not the tone. Notice the conventionalizing of the small, scattered trees on the hillside by using two shapes — the bare stem and the stubby branched tree.
Boston Corners Painting Notes 54, 20 Feb 1920 [NAC]

56 THE GULLY II. Boston Corners, 20 February 1920. Oil on canvas, relined, 51.5 x 61.6. McMichael Canadian Art Collection, Kleinburg, Ontario, gift of the Founders, Robert and Signe McMichael, 1966.16.21.

This drawing combines three of the most important things I have developed in my painting.

1. *The black "cores" of the trees, a convention started in a watercolor, made in 1915 from near Gun Hill Road looking across Webster Avenue to White Plains Avenue. This started from the need of a convention to represent trees looked at against the light where they showed a dark shadowed part surrounded by an illuminated part.*

2. *The softening of texture obtained by washing over a part of the drawing with clear water.*

3. *The use of colored streaks to mark the boundaries of shapes – contours. This was developed in France through a desire to mark the contours of battle fields simply and decidedly. Used notably in the drawings from St Eloi and Gravenstafel. Exhibited Montross Gallery, 1920–21.*

Boston Corners Painting Notes 118, 27 Aug 1920 [NAC]

57 THE POOL, CONTOURS. Weed Iron Mines, near Boston Corners, 27 August 1920. Watercolour over pencil on paper, 28.3 x 39.1. National Gallery of Canada, Ottawa, 3014.

This waterfall thing has always meant a lot to me, a sort of key picture. It fathered the whole summerful of open and shut watercolors made at Dart's. I have always had it with me and it has given me confidence in being able to work over a thing for weeks and get something out of it. It is in oil and was rubbed out and done over and changed and changed and it still wears well.
Milne to Clarke,
24 April 1934 [NAC]

The father of all the summer of 1921 painting, and of many pictures since. This is the "open and shut" motive, simplification by worked over and blank areas. A patiently worked, faulty picture, but it has a "kick" that I have not been able to increase.
Milne to Alice Massey,
15 Sept 1934 [MC]

58 THE WHITE WATERFALL (WHITE, THE WATERFALL). Alander, 28 March 1921.
Oil on canvas (relined), 45.8 x 56.3. National Gallery of Canada, Ottawa, 7156.

59 BLACK WATERFALL. Alander, April 1921. Oil on canvas mounted on masonite, 45.8 x 55.9. Milne Family Collection.

96

The old whaleback is scudding cheerfully before the wind this week – upside down it is true, but making noticeable progress. A painting week – three days rather, so far. . . . Tuesday afternoon worked on the Black waterfall – no longer black owing to the decision when you were here. . . . Wednesday, all day, same continued and picture finished except for minor pruning to allow the shapes to be read more easily. Same as the white waterfall except that here the canvas color – painted on – has been used for sharpening and simplifying. . . . Today, all day until stopped by rain, a new Black Waterfall on a 20 x 24 canvas. Made from lower down, the waterfall zig-zaging from almost the top to the bottom . . . (figure again used, but a little smaller, and not so much camouflaged). . . . The one unsolved problem in it – aside from the details – is the sharpening means. It is absolutely necessary where the red, yellow, gray & green are of same value to separate them in some way where you want shapes to be seen. What I have in mind, gleaned from the sketch, is to use the black outline (this alone doesn't seem to be enough, unless it is heavy) and then not paint the colors on each side quite up to it, so that both canvas color and black outline separate them. . . .

Milne to Clarke, 21 April 1921 [NAC]

60 WATERFALL. Palgrave, June–July 1930. Colour drypoint, 17.5 x 22.6. National Gallery of Canada, Ottawa, 15985.

I got a 14 x 18 canvas and decided to try white alone as the shape sharpener – have used black times without number of course in both oil and watercolor. The day probably had a strong influence in deciding me to use precious hours in trying it – if ever a day called for white paint and lots of it, it was today.

It worked, though I didn't know it until I had finished. Scratched on the colors miser fashion and without any preliminary outline. At this stage it was a bit discouraging, looked very weak and loose. Then I emphasized the shapes by painting in between with white, and it gained decision with every squeeze.

Looks a little like a monotype – quite oily. As a matter of fact it is a pretty good translating of my watercolor method in oil. Gets the same things I try for in watercolor, decision in shape without putting anything down that does not bear directly on that end.

Incidently I nabbed the old stump and chopping log. He looks like a white crowned and robed king with two big beautiful grease spots on his train.

Milne to Clarke,
11 Feb 1921 [NAC]

61 DRIFT ON THE STUMP. Alander, 11 February 1921. Oil on canvas, 35.9 x 46.1. Vancouver Art Gallery, gift from the Douglas Duncan Collection, 70.61.

Creative art (or any creative effort) is life (the highest life of which we know), is human experience – as distinguished from animal life.... As higher animals our chief interest is in reproduction, food, shelter, health – just as it is in the lower animals – our aim is to carry on the race as it is.... If that were all that human beings have aimed at we would still be swapping skins in a cave. It is static. The one thing that has moved the human race, developed it, is creative courage, imagination.... Pictures are merely (material things,) a byproduct of the painter's effort. The important thing is the effort, the striving itself.[1]

■ Milne wrote these words a few days after Christmas 1930. He often drew this distinction between day-to-day survival and creative development, between what he termed existing and living. It is central to an understanding of his personal artistic achievements. For Milne, personal, individual vision was crucial to true creativity; there seemed little point to art if it was not inventive, if it did not add to what was already known. He criticized one author for claiming that

the way out of a difficulty is to use the solution someone else has found, and be sure you are right. Learn to do it as it has been done – craftsmanship – not as it has not been done – thought. Craftsmanship is just second hand (many times over) thought....

Instead, Milne argued, the artist should

Try to load up with a few articles of our own – possibly only a very poor line of tinware but at any rate hammered out with great effort and great enjoyment.[2]

An artist must not simply see as others have seen before him, imitatively; he must, like his great predecessors, discover for himself, revealing sights anew. This "creative seeing, *with effort, work, against one's will, takes courage.*"[3] Art is not "a

technical performance, an accomplishment, a superficial matter of the trained eye and hand," but rather

a way of life, shaped and moulded by influences before the artist's birth, by his training, particularly in the very early years, and by every event and circumstance of his life.... I am convinced that place of birth is of only superficial importance to the artist and that race and family go very deep.[4]

In 1919, Milne, whose own ancestry was Scottish, wrote to his friend and lifelong correspondent, James Clarke, that his current style, using scratched dry colour and large areas of white paper, was "a Scotch motive, getting the result with the slightest possible means."[5] Milne believed that simplificaton and economy of means were necessary to maintain the strength and impact of a work of art, that its power must not be complicated and thus diffused through detail and overworking. In England, he had been struck by three small carvings, one of which, depicting St George and the Dragon,

was the simplest rendering of the famous subject that I have seen. Just enough to show what it is.... You don't stand amazed before them and feel that they were done by an artist – a superior being – you accept them and feel that you understand just exactly [what] the poor dub had in mind when he was doing it. In fact you are quite confident that you could do ever so much better – now that you know how – have the idea.... This comes pretty near being my rule for distinguishing art from junk.[6]

Milne was fascinated by intensive, exhaustive observation. Throughout the decade of the 1920s and into the 1930s, he focussed visually on the landscape around him and verbally – in painting notes, diaries and letters – on his artistic theo-

Creative Courage
Megan Bice

99

ries, techniques and concepts. These years contained neither the beginning nor the conclusion of interests; they offered an arrival at mastery, and a crystallization of ideas and approaches. Ultimately, in his remarkable letter of 1934 to Alice and Vincent Massey, he set forth a declaration of his artistic concerns, a vision which provided fertile ground for the continuing explorations of his later years.

MEGAN BICE

Through all this, it is clear that the purpose of art, for Milne, was its vitality, its growth and experimentation. Art was synonymous with life of the highest order. As he refined his techniques and theories throughout the 1920s, his purpose remained constant. His efforts and goals in his oils, watercolours and prints reflect his deep determination to produce moments of "aesthetic emotion" in his images.

David Milne's artistic ideas were well established in the early New York years, so that by the time of the famous and controversial Armory Show of 1913, "I had my feet firmly planted on a path of my own."[7] His progress continued steadily in the new rural environment of Boston Corners and through the discoveries made on the battlefields of France. Returning to Boston Corners in 1919 with fresh energy, Milne worked in both watercolour and oil. At the same time, he kept a detailed painting diary in which he analysed his use of the two media and his discoveries. Watercolours suggested "doing oil more freely, less laboriously. Tendency in oil to be over awed by slower medium and so work more feebly."[8] The simultaneous, comparative use of the two media continued over the next few years.

Crucial to this process, the building of a mountainside cabin in 1920 was the result of

a bomb in the shape of Thoreau's Walden. I know Wal-

den so I rather felt a rereading might produce an explosion in my mind; I was not prepared, however, for a similar one in Patsy's. As it was, the great idea burst in her mind before it did in mine.

The great idea was that Milne's wife, Patsy, would work in New York over the winter and that the artist, with $200 made "by skinning the unsuspecting picture dealers" in the city, would

build a hut up the mountain and start a primitive winter of painting and writing, swiping Thoreau's ideas of economy and particularly holding to his plan of spending little time on things that interest you very little and that you are not likely to do well.[9]

Around November 1, Milne began construction of the cabin, modelled after the semi-cylindrical army huts at Kinmel Park Camp, a style of architecture compared to which "you will never find anything more comfortable, convenient or healthy."[10]

The retreat to Alander Mountain was not an act of sacrifice or self-denial on Milne's part; it offered him the luxury and the excitement of a life removed from distractions, focussed on art. Why? As he later wrote in his autobiography,

that troubled Clarke rather more than it did me. Perhaps the deciding thing was that I pictured myself living in that sheltered snowy valley with endless painting material just outside my door, or even, as it turned out, from inside the door.[11]

Perhaps as well there was an element of the "Scotch motive" in the decision, not only in the painter's independence of spirit but also in a Presbyterian intolerance of material excess and an emphasis on hard work and the spiritual core of life. He later wrote to the Masseys that he possessed "the taste for few and simple things, extending to an almost abnormal impatience with possessions that go beyond necessities."[12] The real necessity was the freedom to explore the imaginative and creative realms. One can almost imagine the artist nodding in agreement while reading Henry David Thoreau's conclusion: "When he has obtained those things which are necessary in life, there is another alternative than to obtain the superfluities; and that is, to adventure on life now, his vacation from humbler toil having commenced."[13] Milne's life and art were parallel in their stripping away of excess, in their drive toward an intensity of experience.

Milne did find in the view from his Alander doorway the subject of *Drift on the Stump* [61], which "looks like a white crowned and robed king with two big beautiful grease spots on his train." The snowy February day was one factor in "a momentous discovery," that of white paint. Although Milne had been applying "vast quantities" to his canvases, he had not been "making any real use of it." He felt that his paintings were failing

somewhere toward the end of it, the simplifying stage.... I made up my mind very fully that I was slipping on the white – that is in switching from watercolor to oil.... [The use of white] gets the same things I try for in watercolor, decision in shape without putting anything down that does not bear directly on that end.

The artist now suddenly saw white as the "extra color" in his painting supplies.[14] Its use was refined in the seminal work *White Waterfall* [58]. White dominates and defines the composition; the various parts are separated and emphasized not so much by contrasting outline as by the flow and structure of the intruding white mass. *Black Waterfall* [59], painted shortly after, pursued "something of the same scheme ... but tried using

that gray blue for the simplifying pervading color," a technique explored again several months later in *Gateleg Table* [62].

The thing that encourages me most, though, in these is getting something out of the slowness of oil, studying the shapes to the last notch and not catching them as they fly. For instance, instead of drawing the shadow and boundary contours as they appear at any moment, I have been trying to get hold of the shapes and then using shadow and boundary contours to mark them.[15]

The paintings came closer to a more economical translation of the fullness and the interplay of the shapes before the artist's eyes. The use of the white page in watercolour transformed into the manipulated, positive force of white colour applied to the canvas. The legibility of the painting, its readibility, was simplified through the contrast of blank or simpler areas with more detailed and complicated design. For Milne, the speed with which his art could be grasped was paramount; the success of the small carvings in England was that the whole idea could be seized suddenly, almost as a revelation. Distractions, refinements, details – all unnecessary visual wanderings – reduced the impact.

White Waterfall was a breakthrough for the artist. He later described the canvas as

the father of all the summer of 1921 painting, and of many pictures since.... A patiently worked, faulty picture, but it has a "kick" that I have not been able to increase.[16]

It is no wonder that the Alander cabin, to the outsider a situation of deprivation, was a place of wealth for the artist, always fondly remembered. In April 1921, he left, for although "the cabin was a work of solidity ... the enterprise had no economic foundation."[17] A month later, he wrote

62 GATELEG TABLE. Boston Corners or Mount Riga, 15 May 1921. Oil on canvas, 35.3 x 46.1.
Confederation Centre Art Gallery and Museum, Charlottetown, gift of the Douglas M. Duncan Collection, 70-7-1.

to Clarke that "every time I think of the peaceful little untouched unvisited refuge, it makes me homesick,"[18] even commenting from the distance of Palgrave ten years later that "the little cabin keeps a very strong hold on my memory, the most vivid place memory I have."[19]

Milne obtained summer work as a handyman at Dart's Lake Camp, where Patsy worked in the office. The discoveries instrinsic to *White Waterfall* extended into the watercolours of these months.

The overburden of detail was lost and the precision was retained. The Dart's pictures were all in the same vein. They might be described as line drawings in colour. Shape was all important, colour was a mere agent in simplifying the form. The chief means of simplification was form itself, a contrast of open and worked over spaces – open and shut painting was Clarke's name for it.[20]

In *Across the Lake* [73], the "open and shut" contrasts are particularly dramatic. In concert with his painterly interests, Milne sought out subjects which demonstrated unbalanced compositions, an idea in complete opposition to an idealized view of nature. The search shows a fascination with the reality of perception, the "natural seeing"[21] of everyday random arrangements.

The seeking for an empty subject and the unbalanced composition are very much alike. The dropping of any conscious plan of composition, the theory that one subject is as good as another, and that there is no meat in arrangement or balance for me at present.[22]

In the fall of 1921, Milne and his wife moved to a house in Mt Riga. The house was sold in March to James Clarke and the couple lived rent-free in exchange for renovations to the dwelling. In February he wrote to Clarke that he was devoting most of his painting time to oils.

Naturally whatever thought was to come in oil was to be developed from what I have been doing up to then, that is from the watercolor. Whenever I became reconciled to this and contented myself with holding in reserve a particularly warm welcome for anything that might develop through work in oil, I got along better.[23]

He discovered a tendency to use colour and values "as separate weapons" in separating or emphasizing shapes: colour for minor separations, black and white values for major.[24]

Though never described as such, *The Haystack* of 1923 [75] is, in its subject matter, an homage to the painter Claude Monet. The haystack series had been Milne's introduction to the French impressionist and he had been "thrilled by just one thing, his singleness of heart, the unity of his pictures. There was no straying into bypaths." For Monet, subject matter was merely the structure on which to hang painterly concerns. In Monet's various series, "we got no return to the world around him, no story except the barest of recognition. We can tell they come from cathedrals, or bridges or cliffs and that is about all. Their appeal is aesthetic."

Milne also admired Monet's reduction and elimination of visual emphasis, evident in the French painter's revolutionary usage of colour and value. While admitting that his early works showed influences of Monet's style, Milne observed that in his later career these technical superficialities disappeared. The Frenchman's "great effect" was far more profound.[25] Monet had ventured into the aesthetic and ideological regions frequented by Milne.

Milne experimented briefly in coloured drypoint etching at Mt Riga early in 1922. "The possibility of further experiences with texture," "that intimate combination of form and colour," intrigued the artist. "Drypoint particularly, be-

63 TRIPLE REFLECTIONS II. A Dart's Lake subject repainted at Mount Riga, 8 December 1921. Watercolour over pencil on paper, 38.8 x 53.7. Rodman Hall Arts Centre, National Exhibition Centre, St. Catherine's, Ontario, bequest of the Douglas Duncan Estate.

The Dart's Lake drawing of Sept. 19th redrawn. The September drawing was noteworthy because it was the first of the season's drawings to be influenced by the autumn color. The richness of the new and varied color led me to mark the shapes with larger masses of color than was usual in the previous drawings, where a uniformly thin line was used. The second drawing was made to eliminate some confusion in the foreground, and to make more readable the new emphasis. As a rule the development of a new convention is not fully grasped until toward the end of the sitting, that is, until the convention is seen on paper. In this the change in the line — from a uniform line to an irregularly thickened one, fattened, half-way between a line and a string of colored spots — was not consciously thought of until the tree reflections in the lower left corner were on the paper. Those in the lower right were added today, and the convention was used in a slightly different way in drawing the trees and boulders. The vertical reflections in the second pool are a different convention, though arising from the same influence. The thin bands of color are placed directly on the white paper, not between black outlines as in the rest of the picture. The omission of the black makes the color in this area more brilliant, and gives a different texture. It was used more vigorously a few days later in the Dart's Lake drawing with the canoe. The same autumn color, reflected in a still pool in one case and a ruffled pool in the other, was responsible for the development of these two conventions.
Mt Riga Painting Notes 22, 8 Dec 1921 [NAC]

cause of its possibilities in soft and harsh line was an attractive field for experiment." However, without a proper printing press (Milne had commandeered a neighbour's wringer) or tools, "the process never went beyond the purely experimental stage."[26]

In order to submit watercolours through Canada's National Gallery to the British Empire Exhibition at Wembley and in the hopes of setting himself up as an art teacher, Milne moved to Ottawa in the fall of 1923. At first, he was "anxious to see what the change of subject will do" and there were some incipient ideas about "night drawings."[27] Paintings were sent for a large one-man show at the Art Association of Montreal, to a group show at Toronto's Hart House and to Wembley. The National Gallery bought six watercolours. However, Ottawa was an unhappy period. No sales resulted from the exhibitions and the teaching idea fell through.

Ottawa developed nothing. Perhaps I felt too insecure, too much disturbed in mind. Then, when cold weather came I didn't have clothes warm enough for working outside and painting fell away. At that time I wasn't working inside from sketches, everything was done on the spot. Unfortunate. I could have done better with different painting habits. Altogether I showed little resourcefulness in this Ottawa interlude. I never seemed to adapt myself to my surroundings and circumstances, in painting or in anything else.[28]

Of the Ottawa watercolours, which were continuations of the Dart's Lake "open and shut" motif, *House of Commons* [64] is particularly interesting. Details of benches and tables were erased from the work, emphasizing the composition's strong diagonals and thus the deep space of the hall. The abraded texture caused by the erasure may have influenced the artist's decision to

64 HOUSE OF COMMONS. Ottawa, 7 November 1923. Watercolour over pencil on paper, 38.8 x 55.6. National Gallery of Canada, Ottawa, 16438.

Have got permission to sketch practically everywhere in Ottawa. If King – or Lloyd-George – were here I would undoubtedly have permission to make a picture of him by this time. As to the pictures themselves I have made only two – both of the parliament buildings. One is no good and one has some promise. If I stick it out here I am anxious to see what the change of subject will do.
Milne to Clarke, c. 23, 30 Oct 1923 [NAC]

65 E.B. EDDY MILL, HULL, QUEBEC. Ottawa, December 1923. Watercolour over pencil on paper, 36.9 x 54.3. National Archives of Canada, Ottawa, gift of Mrs J.P. Barwick.

66 PORCH AT NIGHT (VERANDAH AT NIGHT I). Big Moose, c. August 1923. Watercolour over pencil on paper, 39.1 x 56.9. Carleton University Art Collection, Ottawa, gift of the Douglas M. Duncan Collection, 1970.21.

Waiting for business like spiders in a web. When we hear a rattle at the dock which is the outermost thread of our web we run out to pull in the victim. We have been thorough about setting our trap. A searchlight that lights the dock, two Japanese lanterns on the walk to the landing and two on the porch, lights in the house. Painted tables about which people enquire — two new ones added this year to the Roman striped one of last. One of the new ones portrays a running deer which someone, not learned in natural history, mistook for a kicking mule. The other is taken from the pattern on the "Blue Dragon" china which the tea house uses. The dragon itself was at once dubbed "an Adirondack Chicken."
Milne to Clarke, June 1923 [NAC]

67 OLD R.C.M.P. BARRACKS I. Ottawa, 8 January 1924. Watercolour over pencil on paper, 39.1 x 56.9. Carleton University Art Collection, Ottawa, gift of the Douglas M. Duncan Collection, 1970.21.

Art life has had only two minutes lately, one when I got a fine color feeling from a green smear on a 2 x 4 that I had scraped over some bushes, the other a matter of perspective. Did I speak to you about the perspective problem in the Mounted Police barracks picture in Ottawa? Curving of upper horizontals due to vanishing in two directions. . . . That had to be figured out. But the same thing in the back of the house with the bare studding was so striking as to be disquieting to a carpenter. I hastened to measure.
Milne to Clarke, 23 June 1925 [NAC]

roughen the surface of the ceiling space. The procedure recalls an idea suggested in notes written a few months before:

Texture, in its effect on color, can be used only in painting. The combination of painting and sculpture is not usually successful. But the development of texture might originate a new art that might naturally be between the other two.[29]

Along the upper edge of *House of Commons*, Milne retained the dark lines of the overhanging balcony. By not moving farther into the room and eliminating this obstruction, he emphasized again the vast dimensions of the room and the position of the artist/viewer in this space. The device demonstrates the interest in "natural seeing," by which "we see past a man's shoulder, we get a momentary glimpse from a doorway; we seldom see things at leisure and clear-cut." Without these obstructing foreground interruptions, "we miss the tantalizing mystery of the original view."[30] In the Montreal oil, *Carnival Dress (Dominion Square I)* [78], the dark lamppost and the row of flags contribute some of the same effect. They visually animate the composition, helping to convey the "very strong jolt" experienced by Milne when he first looked at this scene of "a white winter fog."[31]

Milne felt that the coming spring weather might have improved his situation in Ottawa, but his time there was ended with a suggestion from Clarke. He proposed that Milne return to the Adirondacks and build a house at Big Moose, financed by Clarke, which could be operated by Patsy as a teahouse and eventually sold. Until 1929, Milne's life was to be divided between summer house construction at Big Moose and winters assisting Patsy in the Lake Placid Club skier's teahouse.

The years in the Adirondacks were difficult ones for Milne, with much valuable time consumed by house building and catering to teahouse customers and skiers. He continued for a time to work in both watercolour and oil with simplification through form, colour and value. Although his handling of the oil medium loosened, it is evident from his painting notes and letters that his objectives remained the readability of the image and the unity of disparate shapes and textures. His frustration with one canvas was that "it lacks unity, simplicity, compression – it is a thing of parts."[32] At the same time, watercolours were losing their potency as a companion source of inspiration to painting in oils. In June of 1925, though "spring didn't deserve any such tribute,"[33] Milne painted a *Tribute to Spring* [81]. Despite the novelty of its lively spattering and the fantastical zoomorphic shapes of the tree stumps, *Tribute to Spring* was one of the last watercolours for twelve years. By November Milne found his "thoughts turning a bit to etching as a running mate for the oil and successor to the w.c., particularly my scheme of colored etching."[34] He asked Clarke to watch out for a second-hand press for him. By the late spring of the next year, Milne self-mockingly complained that he didn't know of "anybody's work that is more full of promise and less of performance,"[35] continuing a month later with the question

Did you ever try to break out of your channel & overflow your banks – override your artistic convictions? The economy principle – in the present place the mid-value idea…. I find it impossible to jump out of it. I sometimes find myself trying.[36]

Added to the doldrums encountered in his art was the apparently never-ending construction of the house.

This little patch in the woods where Doc Williams cut his firewood one winter is my choicest outdoor studio. Just out of hikers' reach because off the trail. They can be heard, rarely seen, never see. With various versions of the Caulkins & Holden commission set round on easel and logs I climb up on the big boulder and get a fine plunging view. The boulder itself is a very fine easy chair. Just now versions 1 & 3 wc and 2, 3 & 4 O[il] are propped up. Version 3 O is the top notch so far. . . . [It] has compression but is thoughtless in some details. The whole ground has not been surely figured over. It is jumped at. Today I should have all problems solved and be able to start in with decision and get a bit of speed up, enough to carry me through in a straight line without investigating side paths.

Milne to Clarke,
19 Aug 1925 [NAC]

68 VALLEY, LAKE PLACID III. A Lake Placid subject painted at Big Moose, August–September 1925. Oil on canvas, relined, 40.7 x 50.8. McMichael Canadian Art Collection, Kleinburg, Ontario, gift of the Founders, Robert and Signe McMichael, 1966.16.25.

This thing was too big for us, so far as money goes, too long.... We probably won't get it all cleared up until next June, and we are pretty well run into the ground.[37]

For the artist, "the accidental – in which the opportunity for all creative painting lies"[38] was important in the continuing development of ideas. By 1926, he felt himself to be only reworking old concepts and to be adapting his subject matter to his current art theories. The excitement of discovery was lessening.

MEGAN BICE

Noticed that the deadening was getting serious last Sunday.... Not enough interest to paint or write or even go for a long walk.[39]

Doubtless sensing the despondency in his old friend, Clarke offered to buy a printing press in return for one pull of each edition made. The press arrived in December.

For Milne, the accidental with its discovery and progression, could be found both in contact with nature and through the act of painting itself. The close observation of nature could inspire new ways of thinking. There were two ways of choosing a subject:

1. *Wander around, gradually warming up until something definitely connects with the painting chapter you are in at the time – at present the three values – and sets off the fuse. That gives you an initial velocity that will carry you into the thick of the work, when you can generate your own power as you go.*
2. *Make no effort to see how your subject will connect with your painting before hand – one subject is as good as another.... You start dead cold. This is bound to be harder slower work.... However it has one advantage – it keeps you from getting too narrowly into a net – makes you face new problems and occasionally start a new view.*[40]

The two methods seem to have come together in late summer with Milne's discovery of the Painting Place. With no intention of painting, the artist had set out for a long walk, succumbing to an hour's nap in the hot sun on Gambles Cliff above Big Moose. "The first blink on waking, before I lifted my head, introduced the frame."[41] The strong values of *Painting Place* [2] were a theme to which he often returned, in three paintings, culminating in the version done at Weston several years later, and in several prints, including the massive series done for the *Colophon*.

The arrival of the press from Clarke also brought rejuvenation. Although the first prints were "merely process and the result painful to look at,"[42] the cross-fertilization of watercolour and oil was replaced by that of etching and oil.[43] The etchings often took their subject matter from existing paintings though they are by no means slavish imitations. They thus have some of the analytical quality of Milne's painting notes: questioning, solving and energizing. The fact that the etchings are individual and rarely in true, replicated editions attests to the experimental use of the medium for the resolution of problems and approaches.

In *Outlet of the Pond, Morning* [84], Milne returned to a subject often previously explored: a bank of trees, an open foreground expanse of water and the fascination of reflections. The work combines many themes: line drawing in colour, "open and shut" opposition, the variation in value and marking by colour, and the "dazzle spot." The use of "interrupted vision" (the visual obstacle of "natural seeing"), the blank area and the dazzle spot are closely related.

The blank area must be sharply in contrast with the rest of the picture, and it must be without interest in itself. Its purpose is to engage the attention quickly, and immedi-

ately release it in the detailed part of the picture. It is a transformer, it steps up the speed of grasping the picture and so increases the aesthetic kick; for speed, concentration, is the basis of aesthetic painting.[44]

The elliptical blue-grey ripple on the water's surface cuts through reflected detail and mirror surface alike. A momentary effect, it positions the viewer in time and space, heightening the sensation of sweep across the still lake.

In late January 1929, Milne wrote to Clarke describing his questionable advances in the skills of turning while skiing, with these additional analogies:

The drypoint is a ticklish tool, very much like skis — infinite possibilities but hard to control…. The painting is just about where the turns are. It is time to link the sections up a bit into something more thorough.[45]

With the house at Big Moose finally sold in the summer of 1928 and one last winter spent at Lake Placid, Milne returned to Canada in the spring of 1929. Enchanted by the landscape of Temagami, he camped for the summer months, moving on to join Patsy at Weston, near Toronto, for the winter. In June he wrote that "every year at a certain stage in the season the flower painting impulse is sure to come" and the subject proved a rich lode at Temagami. The paintings done in these months consist mainly of flowers. An exhilarating letter describes the production of *Tin Basin, Flowers in a Prospector's Cabin* [**95**]: the gathering of the flowers, their placement in an interior, the shifting and reshifting of flowers, basins, bottles and water — "the object of the flowers was merely to throw colored reflections on the water and tin" — the cold start, the restlessness, the breaks from the intensity of the whole experience, the lessons from yesterday's

mistakes and the final result — "pretty good." Packing up and returning home, the artist felt

a fine serene feeling…. Soothed, not because the picture was a little better than usual but because I had been away for a holiday, carried into the swing of the thing so that every thing else was crowded out. Very rare in the last few years and even in the last month but coming back again.[46]

The focus and intensity of the solitary months in Temagami must have recalled the peace of the Alander cabin. The flower paintings and the Prospect Shaft pictures are rich in texture and colour; closely observed, they explore the qualities of absorbed and reflected light, the essence of visual perception. The random, almost whimsical effect of *Waterlilies and the Sunday Paper* [**96**] is belied in *Flowers and Easel* [**97**], where the carefully collected still life stands as an autobiographical testament to subject, painting and painter.

The description of the *Tin Basin* experience was a verbalization of Milne's concept of "aesthetic quickening." As Milne later explained in "Feeling in Painting":

Usually, though not always, the painter's subject stirs some feeling in him before he starts work, some warmth, some exciting interest to get him going. As the work progresses, feeling increases. He is quickened by his own activities…. You work easily, rapidly, without halt or hesitation. The pool and its banks and the bush are gone: everything is on that rectangle of paper…. On some rare days the painter can do no wrong, things click into place without conscious effort, difficulties melt away, the picture seems to move under its own power. You are carried along by aesthetic feeling.

For the artist, this feeling, "this aesthetic emo-

69 SERENITY. Palgrave, 1931. Oil on canvas, 46.4 x 51.5. Private collection.

The blank sky as a restful area is the dominating motive. The warmth of the picture — obtained by using a warm red or yellow line with a light middle value — is characteristic of many pictures done about that period.
Milne to Alice Massey, c. 15 Sept 1934 [MC]

70 VILLAGE IN THE SUN. Palgrave, 1931. Oil on canvas, 51.5 x 61.6. Vancouver Art Gallery, Purchase Fund, 58.3.

Almost the same as the preceeding [Serenity, plate 69] except for the sky. The breaking up of the blank area changes the quiet, soothing picture to a vivacious, even restless one.
Milne to Alice Massey, c. 15 Sept 1934 [MC]

tion, quickening, bringing to life," "is the power that drives art."[47]

The winter months at Weston were given over largely to printmaking, reworking and re-examining subjects done previously in oil. However, by spring, the Milnes had to uproot themselves once again, and looking towards the hills of Caledon, reminiscent of Boston Corners and the West Saugerties, the couple moved to rented accommodation in Palgrave. Secure for the next three years in a home and revitalized in his art, Milne was content and focussed, producing works which bring together, with strength and complexity, the various motifs of his artistic philosophy.

In 1934, when Milne wrote to Alice and Vincent Massey offering his entire output of art to date for the sum of $5000, he was separated from Patsy, in need of money and once again living alone in a cabin built by his own hands, on Six Mile Lake. The long letter, in thoughtful and striking analysis, sums up his accomplishments and beliefs. In it, Milne provides a biography and outlines various visual themes, or "motives," which had gradually developed and persisted in his work. He wrote that

motives interlock, and merge, and continue indefinitely. These developments are not planned, there is no definite end and, often, no clear-cut beginning.[48]

The simple statement that "motives may be based on anything in nature," reiterates the artist's belief that one subject is as good as any other, yet equally announces that nature is the starting point for all artistic themes. It is not Milne's intention, however, to accurately copy the scene before him.

The painter gets an impression from some phase of nature. He doesn't try to reproduce the thing before him: he simplifies and eliminates until he knows exactly what stirred him, sets this down in color and line as simply, and so as powerfully as possible, and so translates his impression into an aesthetic emotion.

Many of Milne's Palgrave pictures are views of the town or its individual buildings but his painting subject was something quite different, an experience instigated "by the feeling you get on going out of doors after working inside ... the feeling of light, serenity, everything open above the line of the earth."[49] As he explained to the Masseys, the artist searches in the natural world for the cause of this emotion and discovers "that his feeling came from just one thing, the great restful space above the horizon." In Palgrave, the artist's fascination with the blank sky above the grouped and busy detail of the earth beneath is evident in a work as early as *Across from the Garage*, 1930, and is extrapolated in *Queen's Hotel, Palgrave* [87] and the landscape, *Serenity* [69]. Variations included the reverse, making the "earth & sky all one,"[50] as in *Ollie Matson's House Is Just a Square Red Cloud* [99].

Milne's use of subject matter is complex. Although "your direction is always being changed by your contact with nature" and "you follow where you are led," the development of visual motifs is "not directed by subject, they may start with barns and end – so far as they ever do end – with waterlilies or clouds."

Milne eventually drew his inspiration from realities other than the scene before him. At first, he reworked themes long after the reality had disappeared from view, in the etchings and the Dominion Square or Painting Place paintings. Later in his life, he turned to remembered sights such as lightning or night skies, or to images from books and Biblical stories amalgamated into fanciful themes. The freedom from the immediate view gave him freedom in his art; however, he always retained the recognizable subject. Although he could say, "Love of nature and art are – at least with me – quite separate feelings,"[51] Milne also knew that there was

one thing about whatever I write or paint that has been important so far – an important weakness it would usually be considered. I would consider it neither weakness or strength, merely a direction. The thing is that while I write or paint with one hand I have to have someone – nature mostly – hold the other. I have to have a person to debate with, or an object to paint from or write about.

Milne was infatuated with the physical world. He was spellbound by the variety of individual objects, their colours, their reflections, their textures. His love of close, intense and unjudgmental observation is clear in his letters to Clarke, which inventory the passing world seen from a train window or the trees, rocks, even artist with easel, at a painting site.[52] A recurring idea was "the inventory of the empty house – observing minutest details where details are few."[53]

For Milne, the subject matter, *any* subject matter, whether real or from a book or from the imagination, was the initial reference point. What finally held Milne's attention was the impact, the "jolt" or "kick" or "thrill," received either from the subject itself or later from the act of painting. The artist did not reproduce the landscape; he attempted to reproduce experience. Given his definition of existing and living, Milne's subject in essence was the abstract, the intangible and spiritual, the experiential level of life.

To this end, Milne invented perceptual motifs to convey experience. In the Massey letter, he describes "interrupted vision," one way of interpreting natural perception.

Here is an opportunity for the painter, who is supposed to be an expert in seeing and on whom we depend for all our knowledge of appearances. He can get a kick out of this interrupted vision, and can reproduce his thrill on canvas for those capable of receiving it.

Other themes included the depiction of texture, particularly through the means of harshness and softness of line, as could be seen in the renditions of reflections. The subtlety or power of values and hues was a motif that led to many others. "Open and shut" areas "furnish contrast enough to make it readable."

Important to the portrayal of experience was the revelatory speed with which a painting could be read. Simplification, economy of means, elimination of more than one emphasis all contributed.

Painting is the lightning art, the impact from a picture may be received at one glance. But … it is not instantaneous. Time does enter in and there is always a progress through a picture…. There is no limit to the number of ways of making these paths through pictures, or to the methods, of pulling, pushing, driving, coaxing, of rest and activity, of speeding up or slowing up that the painter may use.[54]

Thus, a favourite motif was the dazzle spot, his "favourite child, and, like many favourite children, a brat, no one loves it except its parent. I believe no one else has knowingly used it." The dazzle spot "throws you violently and quickly into the middle of things."[55] In paintings such as *Kitchen Chimney* [71], *The Water Tank* [72] and the superb *Framed Etching* [88], the viewer confronts blank area, interrupted vision and dazzle spot combined.

Milne's writings were always an afterthought,

114

though they provide an insightful complement to his pictures, both for him and for us, the viewers. They elucidate the language tools of his painting, the vehicle through which he re-created experience. However, Milne was not a purely formalist painter, interested only in perfected combinations of artistic elements. The act of painting, the discoveries made within the physical realization of an idea were necessary to the creative process, as the Wright Brothers' making of an airplane was more creative than dreams of flying.[56] But the finished painting, like the aircraft, was a mere by-product.

Cézanne, I suppose, was the father of that doctrine as in most other things in paint nowadays – you know, leave 'em in the fields – unless you can sell them....[57]

The significance of the creative act lay neither in the initial inspiration[58] nor in the final product; it was the excitement of discovery unleashed by the act of making, the experiential gap between nature and artist, artist and viewer. For Milne, the essential qualities of that experiential space, the purpose of art if you will, were the only two artistic terms

that keep coming back perpetually and are really important. Aesthetic emotion is one and Creative painting is the other. I don't know what the dictionary says – (probably "aesthetic" – see "art," and "creative" – see "God") but my definitions wouldn't suit the dictionary anyway.[59]

Creative courage was the most important characteristic of people, not only artists, who "have created … made a distinct thing – a thing that didn't exist before."[60] Aesthetic emotion, or quickening, was the intensity of discovery, emotional and intellectual, that occurs during the act of artistic creation.

In the early 1940s, Milne responded to a questionnaire:

Art has no objective, an objective is fixed, known beforehand. Art works toward the unknown. That is why it is living not static.[61]

He went on to refer to the sisters of Lazarus – Mary and Martha. The first sat at the feet of Jesus listening to His wisdom; the second scurried about after His material needs, resentful of Mary's lack of assistance. When Martha complained, Christ gently rebuked her with the words that though she was "careful and troubled about many things: but one thing is needful: and Mary hath chosen that good part, which shall not be taken away from her."[62] With this story in mind, Milne set down his definition of art.

Art is love, but not love of man or child, or love of woman, not love of nature or love of country or of mankind. It is just love, love without an object, a spilling of the oil of love. Art is for the Marys, not for the Marthas.[63]

For David Milne, art was the essence of life itself.

The motive most consciously used was interrupted vision, making use of the roof and chimney that cut off a view of the village. Several other motives play a minor part — the blank sky, the white chimney that is not quite a dazzle area because it has some interest of its own, and the use of very dark values. . . . It is interesting to notice that the use of dark values here doesn't give at all the feeling of the later ones, perhaps because the hues used with houses are not brilliant. Milne to Alice Massey, Sept 1934 [MFP]

71 KITCHEN CHIMNEY. Palgrave, 1931. Oil on canvas, 51.1 x 71.5. National Gallery of Canada, Ottawa, 15524.

116

72 THE WATER TANK. Palgrave, c. 1932. Oil on canvas, 40.7 x 55.9.
National Gallery of Canada, Ottawa, 4257.

73 ACROSS THE LAKE. Dart's Lake, 21 September 1921. Watercolour and pencil on paper, 39.4 x 56.9. National Gallery of Canada, Ottawa, 16427.

*Work was steady at Dart's
and so was painting. I worked
in watercolour. Changes forced
by the War Records work and
partial development since
began to bear fruit there. The
overburden of detail was lost
and the precision was retained.
The Dart's pictures were all
in the same vein. They might
be described as line drawings
in colour. Shape was all
important, colour was a mere
agent in simplifying form.
The chief means of
simplifying was form itself, a
contrast of open and worked
over spaces – open and shut
painting was Clarke's name
for it.*
Autobiography, 1947
[MFP]

DAVID MILNE

74 ACROSS THE LAKE (SECOND VERSION). Palgrave, December 1929 and Summer 1930. Colour drypoint, 13.6 x 17.5. National Gallery of Canada, Ottawa, 16065.

75 HAYSTACK. Mount Riga, February 1923. Oil on canvas, relined, 41.3 x 50.8. McMichael Canadian Art Collection, Kleinburg, Ontario, gift of the Founders, Robert and Signe McMichael, 1966.16.26.

120

76 THE BLACK CABINET. Mount Riga, c. October 1922. Watercolour over pencil on paper, 35.3 x 42.9. Winnipeg Art Gallery, acquired with the assistance of the Women's Committee and the Winnipeg Foundation, G 62-14.

77 LANTERNS AND SNOWSHOES (INTERIOR OF THE TEA HOUSE). Big Moose, 4 September 1923. Watercolour over pencil on paper, 38.1 x 55. Milne Family Collection.

Finished the Montreal Winter Carnival. You know it but may not be able to trace it — a black lamp post against a mid value of park, with a string of flags, also mid value, but in color across the top. I got a very strong jolt from the thing when I saw it — a white winter fog. Later I made a few pencil sketches of the trees, flags and post, and rubbed it in quickly in the hall bedroom down on St James St. I had it then, except as Mr Fosbery noted, the post looked lonely. Back in Ottawa I repainted it. The post no longer looked lonely, but I later realized that I had wandered from what I had seen.
Milne to Clarke,
23 Aug 1925 [NAC]

78 CARNIVAL DRESS (DOMINION SQUARE I). A Montreal subject, painted in Montreal or Ottawa, February 1924. Oil on canvas, 45.8 x 56.3. Agnes Etherington Art Centre, Queen's University, Kingston, Ontario, gift from the Douglas M. Duncan Collection, 7-7.

79 SKI-JUMP, LAKE PLACID II. Lake Placid, 1925. Watercolour over pencil on paper, 38.5 x 56.3. National Gallery of Canada, Ottawa, 16437.

80 SKI-JUMP HILLS WITH RADIATING CLOUDS II. Lake Placid, c. March 1925. Watercolour over pencil on paper, 38.5 x 55.3. Vancouver Art Gallery, gift from the Douglas Duncan Collection, 70.64.

81 TRIBUTE TO SPRING. Big Moose, May–June 1925. Watercolour over pencil on paper, 28.3 x 38.5. National Gallery of Canada, Ottawa, 16126.

Sunday went up to the old sawmill. Left my lunch and color box on the kitchen table. Patsy pursued me all round the lake with it and arrived just as I had loaded up with 25 fire bricks (found a new and rich mine) and was starting back. As a tribute to spring I made a speckled (spattered) watercolor. Spring didn't deserve any such tribute. If she had got her just desserts she would have been presented with all 25 of the bricks. Rained, snowed and showed a little feeble sunshine in between. Got home and ate Mrs Day's four pound Laker.
Milne to Clarke,
23 June 1925 [NAC]

82 CLOUDS BELOW THE MOUNTAIN TOPS. Lake Placid, c. 1926. Oil on canvas, 41.3 x 51.5. Private collection.

83 OUTLET OF THE POND II. *Big Moose, c. 1927. Oil on canvas, 41 x 51.*
Milne Family Collection.

DAVID B MILNE Oct 1926 – JAN 1928.

84 OUTLET OF THE POND, MORNING. A 1926 Big Moose subject painted at Lake Placid, January 1928.
Oil on canvas, 41 x 51.1. Courtesy of Woltjen/Udell Gallery, Edmonton.

Shapes are marked by the slightest possible means next to an uncolored line. The drypoint of the same subject is in the same spirit. In both the motive is one of worked over and blank spaces acting as foils for each other.
Milne to Clarke,
Jan–Feb 1928 [NAC]

85 OUTLET OF THE POND. Palgrave, June–July and October 1930. Colour drypoint, 17.6 x 22.6. Milne Family Collection.

Zola is less true to life¹ (less abstract) than Mallarmé. Cormon is less true to life (less abstract) than Klee, but Klee is less true to life (less abstract) than Douanier Rousseau. And Kandinsky is much less abstract than Breughel, Vermeer or Van Eyck: in fact Van Eyck could well represent the extreme point of abstraction in the whole history of painting.
– Jean Bazaine, *Notes sur la peinture d'aujourd'hui* (Seuil, 1953, p 57)

■ In one of the very first articles devoted to David Milne's work, Donald Buchanan wrote:

His paintings are modern but they are not self-conscious. There is nothing abstract in them, nothing cubist, they contain merely the commonplace elements of the Canadian scene.[2]

Buchanan, who had been invited to visit Milne in his cabin at Six Mile Lake on 20 October 1934, was doubtless still in shock after this plunge into nature in the heart of the forest. The painter had recommended that he wear his oldest clothes and get off at Severn Falls station on the CPR line to Sudbury. Milne was waiting for him on his arrival. To get to his tarpaper-roofed hut, they still had to go several miles, partly by canoe, partly on foot, "far from any habitation,"[3] noted the critic, with a few shivers down his spine! But Simcoe County where Milne's cabin was situated had nothing in common with the ruggedness of Algoma, where the Group of Seven members liked to meet.

It was just before Buchanan's visit – 20 August 1934 to be precise – that Milne had given quite a different impression in his famous letter to Alice and Vincent Massey. His intention was to persuade the collectors to buy a large number of his works and, with this in mind, he thought it would be a good idea to enlighten them as to his intentions and manner. About his pictures he wrote:

They don't aim to represent, and have no particular technical excellence, whatever appeal they have is aesthetic. These are not pictures of flowers or fields or houses or jam jars, they have little sentimental appeal; they are simplifications of line and color, intended to produce a thrill, a kick. Many can feel a purely aesthetic emotion in music, few can get it from painting. So my audience, even when I reach it, is limited.[4]

Like all painters who have written a lot about their art, David Milne often speculated about the creative process, the mysterious alchemy which transforms impressions of nature into aesthetic emotions, sensations into painted forms. However, painters today tend not to think of this transformation as something matter-of-fact, automatic. Far from seeing in the painted form a simple replica of a form in nature, they have become more and more aware of the autonomy of the former in relation to the latter. They no longer define art as the simple imitation of nature and the picture as a mere reproduction of the subject. On the contrary, they tend to give more and more importance to the picture in itself and to view it as separate from the subject, if not in competition with it.

It is in this context of thought peculiar to painters of our time that Milne affirms that his painting, if not quite indifferent to its subject, at least does not make representation of nature its prime objective. When he moved from Palgrave to Six Mile Lake, Milne wrote:

It will take time for me to switch from the open skies of Palgrave to the closed material of the bush.... This is a fine chance to test my theory that a change of environment means nothing once you get used to it – that anything is good painting material when you get to know it.[5]

Milne and Abstraction

François-Marc Gagnon

Translated from the French
by Dympna Borowska

F.M. GAGNON

His subjects, which in the passage from his letter to the Masseys he reduced to four – flowers, fields, houses and jam jars (he is forgetting a few as we shall see) – were according to him mere pretexts for more fundamental aesthetic exploration. Milne claims to have chosen them only because they had no sentimental value in his eyes. He was to return to this subject in his diary:

Sentiment is very fine and vital, but in pictures we don't get it at first hand, we get merely an echo, a memory or a day dream, something that has no real existence. Art is not an imitation of anything or a day dream or memory or vision, it has an existence of its own, an emotion we cannot get from anything in life outside it.[6]

It would be difficult to give stronger expression to the autonomy of the pictorial rendering; here sentiment plays the role which subject played in his letter to the Masseys. The emotion proper to painting would be "aesthetic emotion," an idea which Milne borrowed from Clive Bell,[7] but completely integrated into his own system of thought. This emotion is independent of sentiment and may even be in conflict with it. It is born in a mysterious fashion which Milne tried to explain to his faithful correspondent, James Clarke, in his magnificent letter of 3 October 1932, where he asked his reader to imagine he was a painter in search of a subject to paint. When does a subject encountered in nature provoke an aesthetic emotion?

A train passes, leaving a trace of smoke in the sky. This moves you for a moment. "You have often thought of doing something with them," the train, the smoke, the sky…. But it remains in the project stage.

You pass on and come to a mill pond, stand on the bank and look at the reflections. These reflections are your

painting page at the time. A perfect reflection, or is it? No, you decide there must be some unseen movement in the water, some dulling of the image. A slight breeze stirs the surface. The verticals are emphasized, the horizontals disappear, a different image. The breeze increases; the reflection now is a series of vertical bars. More wind and there are only vague shapes of color….

But it is still not right. There is too much wind, "… it will not be a good place to work at reflections that day." Finally, you find the perfect spot, sheltered from the wind but exposed enough for a slight breeze to come every now and then and trouble the perfect calm of the pond's surface; you set up your easel.

Does "aesthetic emotion" arise when the subject coincides perfectly with the artist's plan? In order for the painter to feel it, is it enough for him finally to discover the place ("a corner to paint in") which best coincides with his initial project: to paint the reflections in the water (rather than the smoke of the train passing far away in the countryside)? We are warm, but we are not quite there. You get ready for painting without much conviction at first, continues Milne, the subject only half takes hold of you. You are not yet at the heart of things. Then finally you start to paint.

You open your paint box and start to draw with paint. The going is easier, surer, faster as you go along. You become intensely taken up with the lines on your canvas and the color you plan to fit to them…. The whole world is now in front of you, you work surely, rapidly, you see things you wouldn't ordinarily see, you solve problems that have been simmering for months. In the rare day you can do no wrong, that is aesthetic emotion.[8]

The subject in itself cannot trigger the aesthetic emotion. It is at the moment the artist begins to paint – not even to draw – that the subject and his representation of it become one with each other, mutually illuminating, sources of a specific irreplaceable emotion, "aesthetic emotion."

Milne speculated less about what attracted him to his subject in the first place. In talking of flowers, fields, houses and jam jars, he appears to be implying these things have relatively little importance. He could have painted the smoke from the train just as well as the reflections in the waters of the pond. And yet, the very way he describes his search for the perfect painting place shows that choice of subject is not really so unimportant. A first pond is rejected. Only later does he finally discover the pond where he sets up his easel. For it is less a question of painting a pond than the tremor of wind on the pond, a tremor which gives a vertical slant to the reflection of a subject where verticals have to compete with horizontals, obliques and curves.

Several of Milne's pictures treat this theme of reflection in water. For some, such as *Bishop's Pond in Sunlight*, 1920, this is the main subject they represent. Others include it in a more subtle way, as in *Prospect Shaft I*, 1929 [86], where the subject is simply a prospect shaft filled with water in which the surrounding nature is mirrored, and one really cannot tell where reflection ends and reality begins.

Is it just a subject like any other? I believe not. Milne could have said that, by letting us see reflections in the water of a pond, Nature was enabling us to experience a phenomenon of simplification similar to the one the painter always uses, whatever the subject. In his letter to the Masseys, he did say:

[The painter] doesn't try to reproduce the thing before him: he simplifies and eliminates until he knows exactly what stirred him, sets this down in color and line as

simply, and so as powerfully, as possible and so translates his impression into an aesthetic emotion.

The process of simplification Milne describes is one of subtracting, "eliminating" the adventitious elements in impressions from nature. When Milne was to show his work at Scott's in Montreal in the spring of 1935, French Canadian commentators recognized this reducing process in Milne's painting. Some of them were shocked by it and accused the painter of trying to be original without really succeeding in reaching a wider public.

The subject does not exist as such. The apparent subject is nearly always burnt wood covered with traces of snow set against traces of mud and dry earth and a few blackened buildings. The artist outlines his subjects with black strokes; he makes abundant use of blacks and greys, rather indigestible colours. Is his neglect of tonal values deliberate? Is he colour-blind, seeing red, black or saffron where no one could imagine such colours?…

It is a kind of painting without pattern, without much colour, not requiring much technical skill, refusing to stop at solutions, as it so much enjoys the eternal process of becoming. A fragile, original style, but too frail and personal for Milne to need to try and theorize so much about the "Dazzle Area" or the "Living Value." But his formula may be a source of new inspiration for aspiring artists.[9]

Others were less negative, if not much more enthusiastic. Emile Venne drew attention to the same process of subtraction, but saw in it at least a direction, the possibility of sharing an emotion.

One has to admire Milne's audacity and frankness. He wants to create a dream. It must be stressed that his aim is not just to suggest, to provoke an emotion or feeling on the threshold of the dream, but actually to portray a purely subjective dream. All the art of the painter thus shrinks to a tiny dream, dreamed at a tiny moment, about

*For six weeks or so I painted
some pools in Dan
O'Conner's iron mine — he
says it's an iron mine, iron,
copper, silver, gold, arsenic,
sulphur, molasses — well,
anyway, it looks like a
collision between Winsor &
Newton's and a coal mine,
good for painting.*
Milne to McCurry,
autumn 1929 [NGC]

86 PROSPECT SHAFT I. Temagami, 1929. Oil on canvas, 46.4 x 56.3.
National Gallery of Canada, Ottawa, 15517.

a tiny subject which, for its part, can disappear, as it has nothing further to do with the picture, and is not even the medium or cause of the emotion. So there is nothing but the tiny dream of an individual, something unreal, an infinitesimal moment which the painter must capture in a picture, which will perhaps be only a decoration or an interplay of coloured lines. The astonishing thing is that the result sometimes surpasses this objective and arouses real emotion, which is none the less singularly powerful for being transient.[10]

But what principle guides this work of elimination? Mondrian, who proceeded in the same fashion and finally arrived, of course, at the simple opposition of verticals and horizontals, was seeking the basic structures of the visible universe. I could be wrong, but it seems to me one does not feel such a principle at work in Milne's painting. In my view, Buchanan was right on that point: Milne's paintings "contain merely the commonplace elements of the Canadian scene." If a symbolic function is indeed at work in Milne's painting, it is not at that level.

It seems to me that Milne's painting was capable of self-awareness and that in choosing a particular subject Milne showed himself capable of reflecting on his own artistic practice, which, I fear, would make him a more self-conscious artist than Buchanan believed. One cannot fail to see the profound analogy between painting and subject on the one hand and objects and their reflections in the pond on the other, all the more so as the pond is, as Milne reminds us, having often observed it, a simplifying mirror, a filter, which, in the hotchpotch of nature, retains only the verticals, and then only vague masses of colour. How can one help thinking of him as the "prospector," whose every picture resembles the flooded prospect shaft he leaves behind him, where a fragment of the Universe is reflected?

It might be objected that I attach too much importance to titles. After all, Milne has often belittled their importance. "The Title means nothing and explains nothing. It is merely a handle, a number would do as well...."[11] He has been known to give the same work two entirely different titles. However, in another passage from his correspondence, he not only gives importance to titles, but says he has sometimes created only titles for works which have never left the project stage.

Subject — that is story — has played about as little as possible with me as with anyone I know; yet this [new] direction has to do with subject. More accurately and stranger still, with titles. Titles to me have been handles, recognition words for my own convenience, and fastened on after the pictures were painted, usually when they were sent out somewhere. Now here is one under way that is born with a title, The Alder Branch. Nothing unusual in the title, nothing unusual in the subject.... Absolutely no new motive, but a consciousness of subject or rather of title. There are several others that I have in mind but haven't painted.[12]

He enumerates some of them: *The Trail Worker, The Sunny Stake, A Fish Jump, Two Eggs,* which have in common with the first that they designate more or less regular lines like the branch of a tree, a trail, a stake, the circle made by a fish coming to the surface to catch an insect, or the circles of two fried eggs.

So one must not swear to anything. Titles are less neutral than he believed (or claimed to believe). Moreover, they are less interesting when one reads them simply as ways of designating the subject. They are much more interesting when one sees in them the mark of a concern with the elements of artistic expression, a well-attested concern, of course, in Milne's case.

I agree with John O'Brian when he says that Milne eliminates the symbolic to the extent he eliminates the sublime. But I think he still remained attached to that unique symbolic function which often enables painting today to be a metaphor for itself.

Here is another example, taken this time from the letter to the Masseys which served as our point of departure. Milne was trying once again to define "aesthetic emotion" for the benefit of his future patrons.

On a bright day you go out and stand for a moment: a burden falls from you, you are refreshed, stimulated, uplifted. Why? Just exactly what in nature has stimulated you, the fresh air, the sunshine, the beauty of the landscape? No, none of these! The painter gets this feeling of serenity, just as anyone else does: then something, some timing of his particular art interest at the period, moves him to search out the mystery by painting. In the end he knows that this feeling came from just one thing, the great, restful space above the horizon. He can reproduce his emotion aesthetically by placing on the lower part of his canvas an area of detailed shapes – varied enough to engage and tire the eye quickly – and above this a larger, dominating area, perfectly blank, no detail, no gradation, unteased, unnoticed, without interest in itself, merely an area of rest, a refuge....

So according to Milne the source of "aesthetic emotion" is the paradigm of formal problems with which the painter has to contend at the moment of receiving an impression from nature. Without this network, this decoding grid, he would probably pay no attention to his impression and feel no need to explore its cause. The painter arrives at form, because form is his starting point.

As soon as he understands the cause of his emotion in nature, he knows how to "recreate" it in paint, in this case by contrasting the rather detailed lower part of the canvas with the vast empty space at the top. Milne gives the example of his series *Clouds at the Horizon*, but one could equally well cite some of his architectural scenes, such as *Queen's Hotel, Palgrave*, 1931 [**87**]. Here again, I do not believe any subject would have done as well. Is not this vast expanse of space, this area of "rest," precisely the surface on which the painter works and which serves as his "refuge"? Once more Milne finds in nature a subject which can serve as a metaphor for painting as surface. The pond presents itself as a horizontal surface, like that of the drawing paper, engraving or etching. The white sky, the space above, appears as a vertical surface, like that of the canvas on his easel. I see confirmation that Milne thought along these lines in the fact that in exactly the same context he alludes to Velásquez' *Las Meninas*, and moreover insists on the function of the large canvas in this picture!

The back of his huge canvas shows prominently at one side of the picture, bare, uninteresting. I feel sure many have thought it would be a perfect picture if it weren't for that dull bit. No, it is a greater picture because of it, it is a foil for the more brilliant part of the picture.

Thanks to Michel Foucault, we are more aware that one cannot refer to *Las Meninas* without raising the question of the function of representation in painting. Milne could just as well have spoken about Matisse's *L'Atelier Rouge*, 1911, which, after all, is closer to his style than the vast canvas of Velásquez. As with Matisse or, if you like, Velásquez, the empty parts serve to enhance the parts that are full. Or rather, certain very detailed areas serve to enhance the parts that are blank, which are the true medium for the emotion. Milne does seem to have been much more fascinated by these areas of non-interest, which he

87 QUEENS HOTEL, PALGRAVE. Palgrave, 1931. Oil on canvas, 51.1 x 61.3.
National Gallery of Canada, Ottawa, 15526.

The reflection of the window on the glass of the etching is a dazzle area — a sharp area of contrast of no interest in itself, it merely takes the attention and at once releases it in the detailed part of the picture — it speeds up the seeing.
Milne to Alice Massey, Sept 1934 [MFP]

88 FRAMED ETCHING (LILIES FROM THE BUSH). Palgrave, 1931.
Oil on canvas, 66.1 x 71.1. External Affairs.

138

nevertheless describes with all the pejorative adjectives he can find: "perfectly blank ... unnoticed, without interest in itself," "dull" – as if he were trying to explore a new frontier of art and non-art. But could it not be said that, following the example of *L'Atelier Rouge*, which he knew well,[13] Milne wanted to assert the value of the picture as surface in its own right? After all, Matisse demolished illusionism and perspective in *L'Atelier Rouge* in order to remind people that, before being representations of this or that, pictures – and one sees nothing other than them in Matisse's painting – function in two dimensions.

It is characteristic of the best of contemporary representational painting, when it hesitates on the verge of abstraction, to seek out the symbolic resources of certain motifs in order to reflect on pictorial language. One could cite the innumerable ballet scenes in Degas, where the paintings might be said to put themselves on show; the circus scenes in Picasso's pink period, where the pictures analyze themselves as spectacle; or more humbly here at home, Ozias Leduc reflecting on his art in the still lifes he devoted to his brushes, pencils and tubes of colour, his engravings and his books. The motifs of the pond or white sky in Milne's work appear to me to be of the same order. Certainly these motifs interested him in the first place, but he also saw in the pond's surface stirred by the slightest breeze, or, more clearly still, in the vast expanses of sky above our heads, a metaphor for his own painting.

Milne saw his painting as a constant process of eliminating reality. To Clarke, who had asked him, "Is there any limit to leaving out or putting in of detail provided your large masses are good?" he replied as follows:

I don't suppose there is any limit to the amount of detail that can be put in or left out of a picture. I have one etching this summer based on a last summer's oil, that is half blank, and there isn't much in the other half – yet it works.

My own direction, particularly in the last two years, has been away from details and from the worked areas' sure look that makes some pictures very convincing at least superficially. You get great emphasis from even modelling and you get it from adding detail.[14] The trouble is in modelling you model everything and so emphasize everything – no matter how simple your colors or values may be. Even though detail doesn't break up an area by change of value or color, it takes attention from it by being there. I would say that detail or working areas would have to contribute a great deal to the main idea to justify itself [as] the tendency of all apparent effort. All detail is to increase interest in parts of the picture and so distract from the thrill of the whole.[15]

Although it is difficult to identify the etching he is discussing here, it might well be *Outlet of the Pond* [85], which is from the previous summer and is based on an oil which may also date from the previous summer.[16] Not only does the reflection simplify the motif – Squash Pond in the morning mist – but it is marked by a big blind spot on the right which partially obscures it. Again we are brought back to the motif of the wind creating empty areas in a tissue of reflections.

In reality, on the pond as on the canvas, the forms consist of two elements and two elements only: lines and colours. Are we not very close to abstraction? Particularly as one might say that Milne is driving both line and colour back to the wall.

Still working up to a black outline, but the outline itself is getting a little variety, from fairly heavy to nothing. It is in the nothing direction that the chief interest lies at present.[17]

Pictures usually have more lines and colors than this. Perhaps that is because this one comes from nature at her fastest. If you are to see your lightning picture as a whole instead of in parts, you have just one look, the shortest of looks. Half a dozen lines set in order by three black and white values and one hue, that's all there is. Simple, but not as simple, or as quickly seen, as lightning.
Milne, catalogue for
Exhibition of Little Pictures,
Mellors Galleries,
24 Oct–7 Nov 1936

89 LIGHTNING. Six Mile Lake, 1936. Oil on canvas, 31.2 x 36.5. Mackenzie Art Gallery, University of Regina Collection, gift from the Douglas M. Duncan Collection, 70-18.

Like Cézanne, Milne might have said: "Contours escape me." His line is a contour line which also defines a volume. It marks the outlines of the volume of Ollie Matson's house [99], the forms of clouds, the edges of the trees and hills behind the house, but it is also the hesitant trace of the artist's hand on a surface. Hesitant? Above all fascinated by the appeal of that "nothing," which will finally make this landscape a pure abstraction, dominated by the white space, the great void, above. Has he not already transformed poor Matson's house into a "square red cloud"?

Colour in Milne's work is not used with much prodigality. When he settled in Palgrave he had already reduced his palette to a few tints of similar density: a blue, two greens, a vermilion, a purple. He is generous only with white, and sometimes with grey and black. His recourse to colour is parsimonious: a few spots of red on the house, a little olive green in the small tree nearby, another spot of red at the end of the post on the left, some blue in the V-shaped clouds in the sky. One might say that in Milne's work colour is more denotative than connotative. It is not always justified by a desire to resemble the subject. What is to be done with the dark purple shadows on the Matsons' house in Milne's most famous painting, *Ollie Matson's House in Snow*, c. 1932? They do indicate where the shadows are, but they can scarcely bear any relationship to the real areas of shadow Milne had before his eyes when he painted them. Once again, it is difficult to imagine a less abstract idea of colour.

Nevertheless, Milne avoids speaking of "abstraction" in relation to his pictures. Rosemarie Tovell has suggested that for Milne, a disciple of Thoreau and Emerson, contact with nature was essential. He considered it was this contact which prevented him from falling into repetition and borrowed formulas. In his view the abstract artist, by cutting himself off from this life-giving contact, was condemned to seek inspiration in other painters, thus losing his own originality.

He felt that if the painter's source was not nature, then it must come from other artists, and thus abstract painting was imitative not creative.[18]

It goes without saying that contact with nature does not automatically protect the artist from all such habits, and it can hardly be asserted that no abstract artist has ever been original! In reality the problem lies elsewhere. The problem is to know if a principle of abstraction was indeed at work in Milne's painting, whether or not he was aware of it. If the question is put in these terms, I think an affirmative response is almost inevitable. This principle of abstraction was not the one current in Europe at the time. It was already the one by which American painting was to define its own specific character: not abstract painting seeking to symbolize something exterior to or transcending itself, but painting which becomes abstract because it returns to its own sign structure and questions its own essence. Milne could well be our first formalist.

90 STARS OVER BAY STREET I. Toronto, August 1939. Watercolour over pencil on paper, 28.6 x 35.6. Collection of McMaster University, Hamilton, Ontario, gift from the Douglas M. Duncan Collection, 1970.009.0004.

I don't know exactly what I have been waiting for before acknowledging your letter and check for $50. Thanks for both, I think perhaps I hoped to be able to report some finer grasp of the oil, particularly the finishing up of the "Saint" which I have been doing over a number of times.

Last week I took a day off from it and did a small oil of Eatons College Street, following in the main the color already used in it (in oil) but making changes in it. This worked out better, a one sitting picture. I think, perhaps, I have been doing too much hard work without enough freedom, too conscientious, duty is not an art quality.
Milne to Duncan,
3 Aug 1942 [MFP]

91 STARS OVER BAY STREET, 1942. A Toronto subject, painted at Uxbridge, July 1942. Oil on Canvas, 40.7 x 50.8. National Gallery of Canada, Ottawa, 16600.

92 UNITED CHURCH. Toronto, 1939. Watercolour over pencil on paper, 37.8 x 48. National Gallery of Canada, Ottawa, 6381.

144

93 RED CHURCH II. Uxbridge, July–August 1941. Watercolour over pencil on paper, 38.8 x 52.7.
Private collection.

94 SPARKLE OF GLASS. Big Moose, 1926 or 1927. Oil on canvas, 41.3 x 51.1. National Gallery of Canada, Ottawa, 28429.

146

Again objects are not introduced entirely for their own interest. The new tin basin and plate and the water in them are there because of what they do with the color from other objects.
Milne to Kimball,
Dec 1930 [MFC]

95 TIN BASIN, FLOWERS IN A PROSPECTOR'S CABIN. Temagami, 1929. Oil on canvas, relined, 41.3 x 51.5. Private collection.

96 WATERLILIES AND THE SUNDAY PAPER. Temagami, 1929. Oil on canvas, relined, 51.5 x 61.6. Hart House Permanent Collection, University of Toronto.

148

When I left Ottawa in the spring I went as far north as Temagami, got off the train to look around, and stayed there all summer. Temagami wasn't much different from Big Moose – or Kingsmere, so far as painting subjects went, but it was a nice place to work. I got an old canoe and a tent with a wooden platform and set to work. Once settled I never moved more than three miles away from where I started; that was a reasonable distance to paddle to work. About a third of the time I painted waterlilies, not waterlilies in their wild state as Monet did, but captured and tamed, stuck in pickle bottles, fruit jars and whisky flasks. Even then the waterlilies themselves weren't important, they were just an excuse for having the bottles of water round to diffuse and refract light.
Milne to McCurry, autumn 1929 [NGC]

97 FLOWERS AND EASEL. Temagami, 1929. Oil on canvas, 51.1 x 61.6. In the collection of Victoria University, Toronto.

98 CONTOURS AND ELMS. Palgrave, 1930. Oil on canvas, 45.8 x 61.
National Gallery of Canada, Ottawa, 4258.

There is no division into earth and sky, the white of the clouds is introduced into blue sky, red brick house and green grass, to bind all together in one unit. It depends entirely on the values and hues convention that runs through almost all of these pictures. I have grown so used to it that I am startled when someone, misled by the white, speaks of snow on the ground. Here values are values and hues are hues.

Milne to Alice Massey,
c. 15 Sept 1934 [MC]

99 OLLIE MATSON'S HOUSE IS JUST A SQUARE RED CLOUD. Palgrave, 1931.
Oil on canvas, 46.4 x 56.3. National Gallery of Canada, Ottawa, 15521.

100 THE MAPLE BLOOMS ON HIRAM'S FARM. Palgrave, 1933.
Oil on canvas, 51.1 x 71.5. London Regional Art Gallery and Historical Museum,
London, Ontario, gift from the Douglas Duncan Collection, 70.A.56.

I'm making maple syrup, starting to. Clear frosty nights and warm sunny days, sap is running. Red squirrels climb up and down the little maples licking the trickles that run from breaks in the bark. This morning I loaded the sled with the painting and syrup making outfits. . . . I had to go about half a mile from the cabin, to Rattlesnake Pete's Sugar Bush. Rattlesnake Pete was a Bad Man. Came from the Southern States, and brought with him a peculiar blood-curdling, far-carrying call. Coming home nights he used to call from three miles up the river so his wife would know to have supper ready for him. He went up North somewhere and got himself murdered. He had no mourners, unless his wife missed him. . . . I am Rattlesnake Pete's successor – in syrup making. I have fallen heir to his snowy valley, his big maples and his old sap tins, black now with the bottoms rusted out but still hanging on the trees. I am not sure that Pete ever made any syrup. I see no sign of a fireplace, I think he just tapped the trees and hung up the tins, and went away, shouting, to a better land. I will do better. I will make at least a gallon of syrup. . . . That is the difficulty in this combination of syrup-making and painting – it is apt to produce too much syrup. Painting is difficult, syrup making is easy. I am always thinking the sap is running over, or boiling over, any excuse is good when you are shrinking from the plunge into painting. Today I did fairly well, I was more than usually honest in the division of time. I tapped the bush in the morning and in the afternoon I painted it.
Milne to Kimball, 26 March 1935 [NAC]

101 SUGAR BUSH. *Six Mile Lake*, 1935. Oil on canvas, 46.7 x 61.6.
National Gallery of Canada, Ottawa, 15533.

102 THE WATERLILY. *Six Mile Lake, 1935. Oil on canvas, 45 x 55.*
McMichael Canadian Art Collection, purchase 1983.7.

154

103 THE BIG DIPPER. Six Mile Lake, 1936. Oil on canvas, 31.8 x 36.5.
National Gallery of Canada, Ottawa, 6370.

104 YELLOW COAT. Six Mile Lake, 1936. Oil on canvas, relined, 61.3 x 76.2. Milne Family Collection.

In this last picture of it [the little bay beside the cabin] I wasn't greedy, I didn't take much. On a white ground (snow and sky alike) some patches of vaguely outlined black. Below some of these patches some sharply marked shapes, of trees and driftwood, with a very slight additional emphasis of hues. Everything it has comes from the contrast between the vague unemphasized shapes of black and the sharply defined shapes in which hues are used. It hasn't any title, but you might call it embroidery among patches.
Milne to Graham McInnes [?], April 1936 [MFP]

105 BARE ROCK BEGINS TO SHOW. Six Mile Lake, 1936. Oil on canvas, 51.5 x 61.6. National Gallery of Canada, Ottawa, 16426.

106 SHORE LINE. Six Mile Lake, 1936. Oil on canvas, 46.7 x 56.6.
Vancouver Art Gallery, gift from the Douglas Duncan Collection, 70.62.

158

107 SHORE LINE WITH STUMPS. *Six Mile Lake, c. 1936. Colour drypoint, 12.6 x 17.5.*
National Gallery of Canada, Ottawa, 16080.

Is the shelf picture you speak of the new box with some glass jars in it? I have been particularly interested in noticing what people felt or didn't feel about that one. I liked it. Douglas [Duncan] and Alan [Jarvis] when they were here, wouldn't have anything to do with it. I tried it on Jackson and Lismer and Pearl McCarthy. All were very frank in saying they didn't get anything at all out of it. Then I tried it on Barker Fairley and he liked it. Do you see any reason for this? Well, in looking at Fairley's heads I found difficulty, particularly at first, in getting anything. They were too simple, before I got started at them I was through them, never got stirred up. This picture has the same thing, most people just go through it without having it touch them. Fairley, evidently, is quick on the trigger.

Milne to Schaefer,
16 Feb 1938 [NAC]

108 NEW SHELF. Six Mile Lake, 1937. Oil on canvas, 45.8 x 55.9. Milne Family Collection.

160

Art is not an imitation of anything or a day dream or a memory or vision, it has an existence of its own, an emotion we can not get from anything in life outside it.[1]

■ In 1937, after a lapse of twelve years, Milne took up watercolour again. The medium was to dominate the last years of his career. A list of colours used in the first watercolours of the year – red and black, with small touches of blue, yellow or green – might suggest a narrow exploration of the medium. The work is, however, startling in its execution. In *Red Nasturtiums* [120] Milne uses a heavily loaded brush quickly and decisively. If it were not for the fact that the work also displays an astonishing control, someone familiar with only the drybrush drawings might doubt that it was by the same artist.

Milne described a preliminary version as "a curious double-barreled composition that isn't successful" but felt that there was "a bit of kick in the color."[2] *Red Nasturtiums*, however, explodes across the sheet, recalling the life force of the flowers themselves, and the drawing considerably assists the colour in delivering the aesthetic "kick" which Milne valued.

His concern for clarity is addressed in *The Cross Chute* [11]. The blue water slices across the composition defining space and topography. The vivid use of colour recalls the intense brilliance of watercolours Milne executed in New York, but at the same time the work is as carefully considered as any of the Adirondacks watercolours. In a sense, the watercolours of the late thirties fulfill the promise of the 1925 *Tribute to Spring* [81], a work which combines controlled draftsmanship with an extraordinary overlay of freely used colour.

Given the imaginative power of *Tribute to Spring*, with its multicoloured "snow storm," it comes as little surprise to learn that Milne ad-

mired the art of children. His connections with the schoolchildren of the Six Mile Lake area resulted in a number of works based on children's drawings. The canvas *Picture on the Blackboard* [121] is based on an Easter drawing by two youngsters which was "Thrilling, much better than anything I could do."[3]

In the early thirties Milne became interested in subjects which did not allow for direct painting.[4] As Lora Carney has suggested, his increasing reliance on drawings and memory images as sources during the thirties may have allowed for a greater freedom in Milne's approach to subject matter.[5] He also seems to have established, by the end of the thirties, a working method which resulted in several versions of most compositions.

Goodbye to a Teacher [122] (intended as a parting gift to Miss Cowan, the local teacher), which Milne described as having

one teacher, eleven scholars, one white rat, one porcupine, one robin pulling a worm out of the ground and one small green snake, oh yes, and one almost invisible yellow bird in a tree,[6]

was the product of a long period of thought. By December 1938 the composition had already been painted four times.[7]

The work, "an alteration of vague shapes in opaque color and defined shapes in transparent color,"[8] had been considered "off the paper" since June and had been "at least two weeks 'on the paper'."[9] The process of deliberation is typical; the resulting images are, however, remarkably lyrical and free of any sense of deliberation.

Milne wrote to Alan Jarvis that he "had no thought of character in the faces or figures of the children or teacher"[10] and that

whatever character they suggest was the result of the way the lines fell in drawing the thing in charcoal.[11]

The Late Work of David Milne

Ian M. Thom

161

The fact that there are five extant versions of this work[12] and that the success of the composition rests, at least to some degree, on our involvement in a narrative, suggests that Milne's comments cannot be taken entirely at face value.

The character of *Goodbye to a Teacher* is quite new to Milne's work. A letter to Alice Massey suggests that Milne was aware of this new character.

IAN M. THOM

I have some similar ones more or less planned but have no idea when they will be or whether they will ever be done.[13]

With its naive background based on a child's drawing of a schoolhouse, a yard (which includes a palm tree), and the range of creatures in the foreground, the image is clearly unrelated to reality. It marks the introduction of a new type of painting into Milne's oeuvre – the image is lyrical, even humorous.

Another change in Milne's work was the use of mixed colour. In *Waterlilies in the Cabin* [123] and several other works from the period, Milne makes extensive use of what Douglas Duncan called the "hellish colour." A mixture of permanent violet and yellow ochre, it was used "because it had a neutral look"[14] and had "the feeling of being transparent and at the same time opaque."[15] Brushed, almost absent-mindedly, across the upper portion of the image, the colour unites the disparate elements of the background. Forcing our attention on the dazzling space of the table and the waterlilies, the hellish colour acts as a compressing agent.

Parallel to the changes in Milne's artistic life, there were changes in his personal life. He decided, in the summer of 1939, to move to Toronto to live with Kathleen Pavey (later Milne), whom he had met in the summer of 1938.[16] The shift from the rural life of Six Mile Lake was a dramatic one personally but, as David Milne Jr has noted,[17] the shift in his art was gradual. The "hellish colour" and its gradual change is a unifying element in the work of the period.

Stars Over Bay Street I[18] [90] makes extensive use of the new colour. Milne defined the city through minimal use of line which is allowed to bleed into the wet page. The direction for all the late watercolours is set during this period – wet on wet, with the pigments being allowed to mix on the paper.[19]

The year in Toronto was a visually exciting one. Milne executed several studies of architecture, the cityscape, streets and harbour, domestic scenes which recall some of the New York watercolours, and a fine group of still lifes. *St Michael's Cathedral* [124] is typical of the best work of the period. The matrix of the image is a loose but confident brush drawing to which colour has been applied. The rough application of blue does not define the image in terms of light or shadow, but rather serves to give substance and weight to the building. The subsequent addition of the orange suggests the richness of the glass windows but is not specific. The image as a whole is a remarkable balance of painted and unpainted, defined and vague areas, controlled line and free application of paint.

There are virtually no oil paintings from the period 1938 to 1940. *Chocolates and Flowers* [125] is, therefore, particularly interesting. The work rests on an unnatural colour scheme. The image is one of notable confidence, space being defined only by the placement of objects, a few minor shadows and a single horizontal. There is no difference in the treatment of the table surface and the wall. The architecture of the image is dependent on the varying whites of the background and the single tone used to depict flowers, box and refracted light in the glass bowl. The image reveals itself slowly, but only because Milne felt that the work required a slow fuse. The subtle tension between the quietude of the subject and the scrubbed brushstrokes of the background engages the viewer just as surely as it engaged the artist.

Although the year in Toronto had been a happy and fulfilling one, the Milnes moved from the city that fall. Uxbridge, where Milne soon had a studio on the main street, became his home for most of the next decade. It was to be a period of great personal happiness and a time of what Rosemarie Tovell has called "maturity and elaboration" in his art.[20]

The subjects Milne essayed in Uxbridge were familiar ones: the landscape or townscape, still life, and the fantasy or "subject" pictures. Earlier themes were also revisited in the drypoints and, occasionally, in watercolour.

Winter Comes Softly [109], a view of the street from Milne's second floor studio, is one of several versions of this subject executed in 1940–41. A gentle image, balancing the use of line and wash, it recalls *St Michael's Cathedral* in the use of colour to provide weight to the architecture without dogmatically directing the viewer.

The measure of Milne's distance from earlier watercolours is seen in *Still Water* [111], from early 1941. Milne returns to the theme of reflections but the result is of a character radically different from the images of Bishop's Pond. In a letter to Carl Schaefer, Milne described his goals in this work and the process by which he attained them.

I seem to have a weakness for textures, not imitative textures but such things as contrasts of harsh and soft lines as in this. The idea was to translate the far shore of trees in the fall with their reflection in water into a texture

change. The upper band is done with thin lines of black mostly, with some yellow, warm red, cold red and green, hardly any emphasis in it. The reflections are drawn in the same way, then washed over with clear water and the black and colors added in places while the paper was still wet.[21]

The decision to amplify the reflections by working over the lines while the paper was still wet gives the image a richness we have not seen before. The crisp drawing of trees on the shore is a counterpoint to the soft lines of the reflections. The inky reflections – shadows of the stumps – give definition to the expanse of the water. The image as a whole has a wonderfully accidental aspect to it and yet, as we know, Milne controlled the composition rigorously. This work is "the fourth painting of one started at Six Mile Lake"[22] and "had to be 'read' from left to right."[23] The eye is carefully directed to move "across the composition in a measured rhythm."[24] Our progress into the space of the work is similarly controlled; incident in the foreground leads to the middleground of the reflection and, finally, to the far shore.

The composition, with the rich burr-like line of the reflections, suggested a print to Milne. *Still Water and Fish (First Version)*,[25] which reverses the composition, does not preserve the clarity of the watercolour. A second version [112][26] restores the left-to-right reading and, despite eliminating the stumps, the controlled movement into space.

In the spring of 1941, while awaiting the birth of his son David, Milne evolved the ideas for two of his most remarkable subject pictures, *Snow in Bethlehem* [129] and the series *King, Queen and Jokers* [133]. The genesis of *Snow in Bethlehem* is first described in a letter to James Clarke.

I must have told you about things I have had in mind for

109 WINTER COMES SOFTLY (FIRST SNOW II). Uxbridge, December 1940.
Watercolour over pencil on paper, 37.5 x 55.3. Private collection.

164

Maybe it wasn't really the first snow storm, but anyway there are half a dozen or so snowflakes in it. The oil naturally follows the watercolour so far, or attempts to. However you soon strike impossibilities and have to modify the method a bit for the new medium. So far the change hasn't been as difficult as I expected. Maybe because the watercolours done here lean a little toward oil — that is they are softer and richer, not so harsh and with less black and white.

Milne to Duncan,
21 Dec 1940 [MFP]

110 MAIN STREET. Uxbridge, 27 January–14 May 1942. Colour drypoint, 17.5 x 22.8.
National Gallery of Canada, Ottawa, 16090.

I seem to have a weakness for textures, not imitative textures but such things as contrasts of harsh and soft lines as in this. The idea was to translate the far shore of trees in the fall with their reflections in water into a texture change. The upper band is done with thin lines of black mostly, with some yellow, warm red, cold red and green, hardly any emphasis in it. The reflections are drawn the same way, then washed over with clear water and the black and colors added in places while the paper was still wet. I used to use much the same thing many years ago at Boston Corners. There the drawing was done much the same and a wash of clear water washed over the reflected part, no color added on the wet paper. The soft effect was got by the blurring of lines and edges when washed over with water. I have tried this method lately without result. I know now that it worked then only because I was using very dry color which dissolved and spread a little when wet. The line I use now won't do that, hence the color added to the wet paper.

Milne to Schaefer, 13 Jan 1941
[NAC]

111 STILL WATER. A Six Mile Lake subject, repainted at Uxbridge, 14 January 1941.
Watercolour over pencil on paper, 38.1 x 50.5. National Gallery of Canada, Ottawa, 16121.

166

years and never got to. They sound like subject pictures and maybe are, but not so much as they sound. One or two have got themselves done recently in watercolour and tried in oil. Two of them came from finding books in the library with pictures of old playing cards and snow crystals. I made some outline drawings from them and this fall used them in some pictures. The snow crystals one is "Snow in Bethlehem." It started with the desire to use snow crystals in a picture. It couldn't be realistic since we don't usually see snow as crystals. Hence the Bethlehem instead of Toronto or Six Mile Lake. With Bethlehem it was no trouble at all to dip into eastern architecture from pretty well anywhere in the east. The crystals are spread with fair regularity all over the picture, carefully avoiding the architecture. The chief architectural treasure is a large red church with pinnacles and domes. It really came from a photograph of a church in Tallinn in Estonia or somewhere there, but it does very well for Bethlehem. Then there is a square building with small towers and an arched doorway, my idea of Moorish probably a reminiscence of Omar Kuyam or maybe Beau Geste. Several of these — one with a particularly Moslem look because it has a minaret — showed only dimly because a bit of the sky washed over it, but it is there. Another has a distinctly Anglican look, one of the smaller Canadian chapels — if the Anglicans have chapels. There is also what I think of as a Turkish [cemetary]. I don't know why, there is only a fence with four christmas trees at the corners and a larger one in the middle....[27]

The work has an air of whimsy, a humour, seen earlier in *Goodbye to a Teacher*, which seems to contradict Milne's position as a formalist painter.[28] How is one to account for these works? Is *Snow in Bethlehem* "a metaphor of gratitude"[29] for the birth of Milne's son? Should we take Milne's diffident disclaimer that these works were "not so much" subject pictures as settling the issue?

The question, like Milne himself, is complex.

The fact that this image was redone several times seems to support a formalist reading of the work as an exercise in compositional problems – colour, line, texture. Milne's own statement that he had had such images "in mind for years" suggests a more personal reading and an iconography for the work.

Lora Carney has suggested that in producing the subject pictures Milne, far from abandoning his modernist principles, was widening them to embrace "imaginative human content."[30] This combination of formal, aesthetic concerns and emotional content is, however, not new in Milne's art. The identity between the content and the architecture of the image is seen earlier in the War Records work. The subject pictures recall the earlier work in that they address a specific experience directly. There seems little doubt, however, that the experience is now Milne's own.

Scholars have related the increased frequency of religious subjects to Milne's own religious feelings.[31] While *The Saint* [131] and *Noah and the Ark and Mt Ararat* [130] have the same sense of fun found in *King, Queen and Jokers*, the images of the *Ascension* [134, 135] are moving expressions of a belief in God.

Milne's watercolours from the forties are amongst his most extraordinary achievements. In luminous washes floating across the page, or the rich, velvety blacks of images such as *Yonge Street (Scaffolding IV)* [116], Milne has come close to his

desire to set things down with as little expenditure of aesthetic means as possible ... to wish them on without any material agent.[32]

This grace and fluidity is, however, a product of exceptional skill.

Throughout the decade, Milne continually

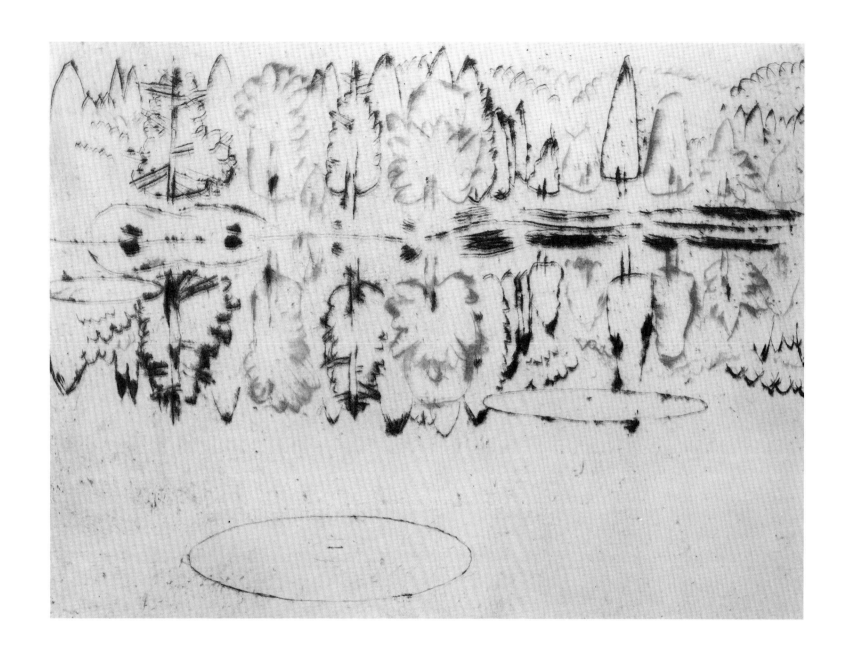

112 STILL WATER AND FISH (SECOND VERSION). Uxbridge, 18 March–8 April 1941.
Colour drypoint, 17.5 x 22.9. National Gallery of Canada, Ottawa, 15959.

challenged himself as a painter. Formal problems were addressed repeatedly and often in a variety of media. The *Stars Over Bay Street* series explored the use of "a light sky and dark buildings" or "a dark sky and bright buildings"[33] in oil, watercolour and a challenging print. Milne attempted to stretch his technical means to bring his prints parallel to the oils and watercolours. The print may be, as Tovell has suggested,[34] a failure, but Milne's willingness to take risks is to be admired.

By 1947, Milne was restless in Uxbridge. He moved himself to Baptiste Lake, initially camping and, the following year, building a cabin. Painting, although it remained paramount in Milne's mind, progressed little. *Shelter at Night I* [117], an early Baptiste Lake work, recalls the vigour of *The Cross Chute*.[35] The precise placing of blocks of colour to build the whole composition testifies to Milne's skills as a builder of images.

Upon completing his cabin, Milne returned quickly to the use of washes in paintings such as *The Lake* [118] and *Spider Bridge III* [119]. Of works such as these he wrote,

The planning has to be done before-hand in great detail; the order in which the colours are to be applied, what brushes are to be fully charged and what with only the slightest amount of paint on them, what effects of the diffusion, spreading and overlapping, due to the wetness of the paper.[36]

Great concentration was required before the burst of activity which achieved the painting which already existed in Milne's head. Ironically,

"Milne found he was sometimes barely warmed up before the picture was finished"[37] and often repainted the subject in order to obtain the aesthetic "kick" for himself.

The magisterial series *Storm over the Islands I–IV* [145–148] which was painted alternately with the *Lighted Streets* [149] watercolours, is Milne at the height of his powers as a watercolourist. The variety of colour, line and form is startling but what is more striking is the intensity of the image. The storm is almost palpable. The aesthetic and emotional realms are united.

In November of 1952, Milne had a stroke which brought his painting career to an end. It is perhaps ironic that what may have been the last painting of his career,[38] *Tempter with Cosmetics III* [150], is a *vanitas* subject. Milne, who had undergone surgery for stomach cancer in 1951, could not be faulted for reflecting on the frivolities of humanity.

Milne once characterized science as "purely intellectual," religion as "emotional but not logical" and art as "emotional [and] intellectual, the emotional dominant."[39] The intellectual, the clarity of his thought is, perhaps, self-evident. Few artists, in analyzing their own work, are as cogent as Milne.

The emotional aspect of art was the excitement of the aesthetic "kick," the intensity of "intransitive love"[40] and "creative courage."[41] It is Milne's ability to combine the intellectual and the emotional aspects of art (together with a complete command of his means) which makes his work so eloquent.

113 GULLS AND LIGHTHOUSE II. A Toronto subject, painted at Uxbridge, 1942.
Watercolour over pencil on paper, 37.5 x 54.9. Private collection.

114 RITES OF AUTUMN III. Uxbridge, 1943. Watercolour over pencil on paper, 37.5 x 55.6.
National Gallery of Canada, Ottawa, 4604.

Alternative titles:
"In Loving Memory" or
"There, damn you".
Milne to Duncan,
3 July 1945 [MFP]

115 R.I.P. II. Uxbridge, 1945. Watercolour over pencil on paper 27.3 x 36.9. Collection of McMaster University, Hamilton, Ontario, gift from the Douglas M. Duncan Collection, 1970.009.0003.

Quote (D.B.M.) *"Use of greenish rather than brownish grey most interesting point to me. Third version — rt. side — a little weak. That's where the colour ran out."* Personal view. If the colour hadn't run out the blame thing would have blown up.
— Kathleen Milne,
Notes on Paintings,
10 Nov 1946 [MFP]

116 YONGE STREET (SCAFFOLDING IV). Uxbridge, 10 November 1946. Watercolour over pencil on paper, 36.5 x 54.3. Rodman Hall Arts Centre, National Exhibition Centre, St. Catherine's, Ontario, bequest of the Douglas Duncan Estate.

In time this shelter may seem almost as good as the one I had when the [Six Mile Lake] cabin was being built, where I could cook, eat, sleep, read, tend the fire, and almost everything else there was to be done without moving from the seat – bed, table, lounge. This place is almost as small, just six feet long and about five wide with the fireplace nearly two feet inside it. It is almost entirely enclosed, all except a little at the stove pipe and some under the roof at the stove pipe side. Living and painting could hardly be done without it this time of year.
Milne to Kathleen Milne, 27 Sept 1947 [MFP]

117 SHELTER AT NIGHT I. Baptiste Lake, 7 October 1947. Watercolour over pencil on paper, 35.6 x 50.8. National Gallery of Canada, Ottawa, 6378.

118 THE LAKE (BRUSH FIRE II). A Baptiste Lake subject, painted at Uxbridge, c. March 1948.
Watercolour over pencil on paper, 48.6 x 66.1. Private collection.

119 SPIDER BRIDGE III. A Kinmount subject, painted at Baptiste Lake, 1950. Watercolour over pencil on paper, 36.9 x 55.6. National Gallery of Canada, Ottawa, 16129.

120 RED NASTURTIUMS. Six Mile Lake, 1937. Watercolour over pencil on paper, 35.6 x 52.7. National Gallery of Canada, Ottawa, 16429.

At Easter when I stopped in at the school the teacher asked me to draw an Easter picture on the board. I wouldn't, so she got her two youngest pupils to do one. Katherine and Norma, each six. The next time I went over I saw it. Thrilling, much better than anything I could do. I have used it in a picture. Made a pencil sketch then worked on it in the cabin, did it over more than half a dozen times and this week finished it. The blank space at the side is just space, to give order and serenity to the picture. The shape at the upper right is from a table of temperatures the teacher had there. The rest is the children's picture — a sunset, with the school, two branching trees, three children, a road, a bird in one tree (looks like a spider but the teacher was told it's a bird), part of a river, a pool and a sail boat — the kind children make out of folded paper. The only kind Katherine and Norma have seen.

Milne to Alice Massey, 1 July 1937 [NAC]

121 PICTURE ON THE BLACKBOARD. Six Mile Lake, 1937. Oil on canvas, 46.7 x 68.3. Milne Family Collection.

178

After dinner I tightened the ski harness, ready for tomorrow and then wrote some letters. In between times I looked at the picture on deck at present, "Good-bye to a Teacher." I have painted it four times now and it will have to get at least one more painting. It looks fairly promising, an alternation of vague shapes in opaque color and sharply defined shapes in transparent color. I have enjoyed doing it, even doing it over so often. It is just a 15 x 21 watercolor but I have spent at least two weeks 'on the paper' and an indefinite time, since last June 'off the paper'. Oh well, that's the way we wear our lives away, we wouldn't be any happier if we were in our right minds.
Milne to Schaefer,
30 Dec 1938 [NAC]

122 GOODBYE TO A TEACHER III. Six Mile Lake, January 1939. Watercolour over pencil on paper, 38.1 x 55.9. National Gallery of Canada, Ottawa, 16432.

In all but the first painting I used a new color, one of a series I have been using – making of course – all getting their quality from an imperfect mixture of two colors of which one is always permanent violet – permanent violet and light red, permanent violet and yellow ochre, and now, in this one and one other recent one [Goodbye to a Teacher, plate 122], *a light variety of permanent violet with yellow ochre. This last particularly has a peculiar quality. Besides the changing look it has the feeling of being transparent and at the same time opaque. It is brushed, not flowed on and so does not define, merely emphasises a shape. Though everything from yellow to magenta shows in it, the effect is rose, a peculiar opaque rose.* Milne to Jarvis,
15 Jan 1939 [MFP]

123 WATERLILIES IN THE CABIN. Six Mile Lake, 1939. Watercolour over pencil on paper, 35.6 x 50.8. National Gallery of Canada, Ottawa, 16431.

124 ST MICHAEL'S CATHEDRAL II. Toronto, April 1940. Watercolour over pencil on paper, 37.8 x 43.5. Art Gallery of Ontario, Toronto, L69.38.

Did the oil of the flowers the day before yesterday and changed it a little yesterday. Very much as planned. There are the usual differences between oil and watercolors as I use them. The first thing noticeable is that the watercolor is much harsher, has more of a black and white feeling. The white of the paper is whiter and the colors appear darker mostly. The second is that the whites have quite a different effect in the oil because two whites are used, a white and a near white, both having the feeling of white. Third, lines are usually more clear cut in watercolor, the color is used thicker and with brushes that are not so pointed. The different surfaces too contribute to this. In general the oils are soft and rich, the watercolors harsh and brilliant.

Painting Notes,
4 June 1940 [MFP]

125 CHOCOLATES AND FLOWERS. Toronto, 2–3 June 1940. Oil on canvas, 45.8 x 55.9. Milne Family Collection.

126 DUTCHMAN'S BREECHES. Toronto, c. June 1940. Watercolour over pencil on paper, 29.2 x 39.4. Vancouver Art Gallery, transfer from the VAG Women's Auxiliary Provincial School Loan Scheme, 65-34.

128 STARS OVER BAY STREET, DARK VERSION. A Toronto subject, painted at Uxbridge, October 1941.
Oil on canvas, image 48.3 x 61.3, canvas 51.5 x 61.3. Milne Family Collection.

127 MUDDY DON. Toronto, 18 June–1 July 1940. Watercolour over pencil on paper, 38.5 x 53.1. Private collection.

129 SNOW IN BETHLEHEM. Uxbridge, 11 August 1941. Watercolour over pencil on paper, 39.1 x 55.9.
Art Gallery of Ontario, Toronto, 2595.

The first of these subject pictures painted, though not the first planned, was "Snow in Bethlehem." It came about this way.

In the Public Library I was looking at an exhibition of books in the central room. One had photographs (I suppose photographs) of snow crystals, always interesting to me, probably as a result of childhood experiences. Interesting but not of much use in a picture since we rarely see them as a part of any scene. I had a feeling that I would like to paint them so I copied a couple of dozen types in pencil. Later I looked at them, probably realized they wouldn't fit in any realistic picture. Connected them with Christmas time in some way (I am not sure of the train of thought), so with Bethlehem. Then the picture was formed almost complete in my mind. Since the subject was entirely fanciful I didn't concern myself with the Bethlehem of history but only with my idea of it. A photograph of a church in Riga or somewhere in the Baltic States was the basis of the large church in it. Some of the others came from my general idea of eastern churches — mosques. One also comes from some idea of a rural Anglican church and one from what I seemed to think was correct for a Turkish cemetary (with an iron fence around it). The hills — I had a vague idea Bethlehem was in the hills. The colour — the dull grey of an early snow modifying the brighter colour of the churches. The snowflakes black and white to avoid confusion with the background. I made a slight pencil sketch, drew and painted the picture from it. Then painted it again with only slight changes.
Milne to Schaefer, 17 Oct 1943 [NAC]

I am doing a "Noah and the Ark," and Mt Ararat! In fact I have done it three times with no luck and I have it drawn again. . . . It is an adventure in understatement, in restraint — some people would call it in confusion perhaps. Noah and the Ark are about the smallest things in the picture, and Mt Ararat isn't very big. Most of the picture is a sort of disorderly procession of animals. . . . The largest . . . is an elephant, confronting a very small mouse on wheels. Behind him two monkeys mounting a ladder. Then a polar bear with his front feet in a small pool, going out of the far side of the pool four fish and a whale. There are two giraffes, two pigs, a cow, a bull, a measuring worm, a chipmunk, a porcupine, a racoon, two wolves following two sheep, a cat facing a dog, a lion with a feeding bottle, a rabbit on a tortoise, a rooster struggling with a baby chick for a worm. This doesn't come under the heading of humor. The point is to make them sharply recognizable and nothing more. They have to be kept in the head if you are to be able to grasp the thing as a whole, because they are so slight and so under emphasised that one is lost as soon as you go on to the next group.
Milne to Clarke, 10 Dec 1941 [NAC]

I can't make out from the descriptions of the pictures whether you have gone surrealist or if you have finally taken to drink or what. I sure would like to see some of those things you describe but I can't get up there and you can't bring them to N.Y.
Clarke to Milne, 23 Dec 1941 [MFP]

130 NOAH AND THE ARK AND MT ARARAT IV. Uxbridge, 10 January 1942. Watercolour over pencil on paper, 38.4 x 56.6. National Gallery of Canada, Ottawa, 16131.

131 THE SAINT I. Uxbridge, June 1942. Watercolour over pencil on paper, 38.1 x 55.3.
In the Collection of Victoria University, Toronto.

132 EATONS, COLLEGE STREET. A Toronto subject, painted at Uxbridge, December 1942. Watercolour over pencil on paper, 28 x 38.1. Milne Family Collection.

133 KING QUEEN AND JOKERS V. Uxbridge, 1944. Watercolour over pencil on paper, 55.6 x 76.7. Art Gallery of Ontario, Toronto, 2781.

134 ASCENSION I. Uxbridge, 1943.
Watercolour over pencil on paper,
55.6 x 37.8. National Gallery of Canada, Ottawa, 16515.

None of the subject pictures I tackle have any
particular point – that is social or political point.
They are not criticisms. They accept without criticism
or purpose, a story or situation or appearance. Of
course others might read something into them though
it isn't there. The majority of painters probably had
something of this attitude, even the painters of church
pictures. Whatever their religious views were, they
probably had little bearing on their choice or handling
of subject.
Milne to Duncan, 20 April 1944 [MFP]

135 ASCENSION IX. Uxbridge, c. 1945.
Watercolour over pencil on paper,
53.7 x 36.9. Private collection.

136 MONKEY AND ORANGE LILIES. Uxbridge, August 1944. Oil on canvas, 38.5 x 51.5.
Milne Family Collection.

I have come out to the bush today leaving Wyb [Kathleen Milne] & David at home on account of the scorching dusty roads. The house isn't bad except at bed time. There is usually a little breeze. David not quite satisfied that all is above board in this postponing of his picnic. . . . We have discovered that his idea of painting is house painting not picture painting. I borrowed his monkey to take over to my place to paint. When he discovered that I had made a picture of it instead of painting the monkey over, he was disappointed.
Milne to Duncan,
5 Aug 1944 [MFP]

137 PANSIES AND YELLOW BOX. Uxbridge, June 1945. Oil on canvas, 30.5 x 40.7. Milne Family Collection.

138 EARTH, SKY AND WATER I. A Coboconk subject, painted at either Coboconk or Uxbridge, autumn 1944. Oil on canvas, 30.2 x 40.3. Milne Family Collection.

196

139 EARTH, SKY AND WATER. A Coboconk subject, painted at Uxbridge, November 1944. Watercolour over pencil on paper, 27.3 x 37.5. National Gallery of Canada, Ottawa, 16490.

140 GLASS CANDLESTICK. Uxbridge, June 1946. Watercolour over pencil on paper, 37.2 x 54.9.
Collection of Mira Godard.

Flowers and art have for us, or some of us, a complete and real existence – servants of none, aids to nothing. In our love of art and love of roses we build our own thin canvas, we accept the imperfect world around us, we must, but within it we build our own perfect world, asking no one's leave, and doing a duty to none.
Autobiography, 1947
[MFP]

141 OIL CAN III. Uxbridge, 1948. Watercolour over pencil on paper, 36.2 x 54.6. Private collection.

142 CAMPFIRE IN WINTER. Uxbridge, c. 1946. Oil on canvas 30.2 x 40.3. Milne Family Collection.

143 FROM THE CABIN DOOR. Baptiste Lake, 21 March 1950. Watercolour over pencil on paper, 36.9 x 54.9. Private collection.

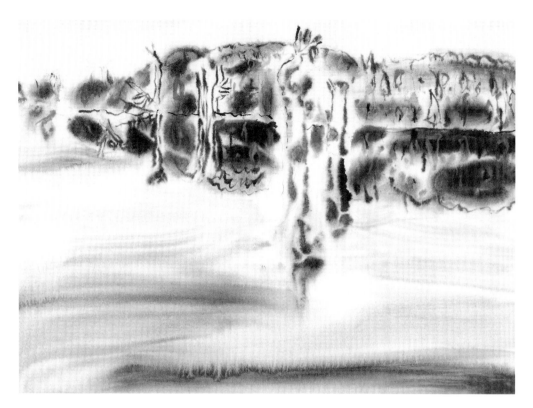

These two small pictures [Storm Over the Islands *and* Lighted Streets], *11 x 15 watercolours. Each is done in a single operation. Everything is planned and the colour prepared, brushes charged; then the paper is wet all over with a large brush. The painting is all done before the paper dries, 3 or 4 minutes, and not touched again. That doesn't make it any easier. The planning has to be done beforehand in great detail: the order in which the colours are to be applied, what brushes are to be fully charged and what with only the slightest amount of paint on them, what the effect of the diffusion, spreading and overlapping, due to the wetness of the paper. Strangely enough that doesn't make the pictures rigid, just the opposite, the whole thing is fluid, easy looking, when completely successful it looks effortless, easy. I remember talking to Cleeve Horne years ago up on Six Mile Lake. His idea was that the whole thing was chance, which is about as far away as you can get. Freedom but not much chance, when one of them is done over a number of times there is very little difference between one version and the next — unless it is deliberate. Yet, if 6 or 8 versions are painted, and set up beside each other a development is quite noticeable from one to the other. Though each repainting is fully planned in advance, the subject is developed as you go along, each version suggests a modification of the plan in the next.*
Diary, 16–17 Nov 1951 [MFP]

144 QUIET RIVER. Baptiste Lake, 15 October 1950. Watercolour over pencil on paper, 36.5 x 54.3. Glenbow Museum, Calgary, gift of Douglas M. Duncan Estate, 70.22.14.

145 STORM OVER THE ISLANDS I. Baptiste Lake, 10–17 November 1951. Watercolour over pencil on paper, 27.7 x 37.2. Art Gallery of Windsor, Ontario, bequest of Frances Duncan Barwick.

146 STORM OVER THE ISLANDS II. Baptiste Lake, 10–17 November 1951. Watercolour over pencil on paper, 27.3 x 37.2. Art Gallery of Windsor, bequest of Frances Duncan Barwick.

147 STORM OVER THE ISLANDS III. Baptiste Lake, 10–17 November 1951. Watercolour over pencil on paper, 28.0 x 36.9. Art Gallery of Windsor, bequest of Frances Duncan Barwick.

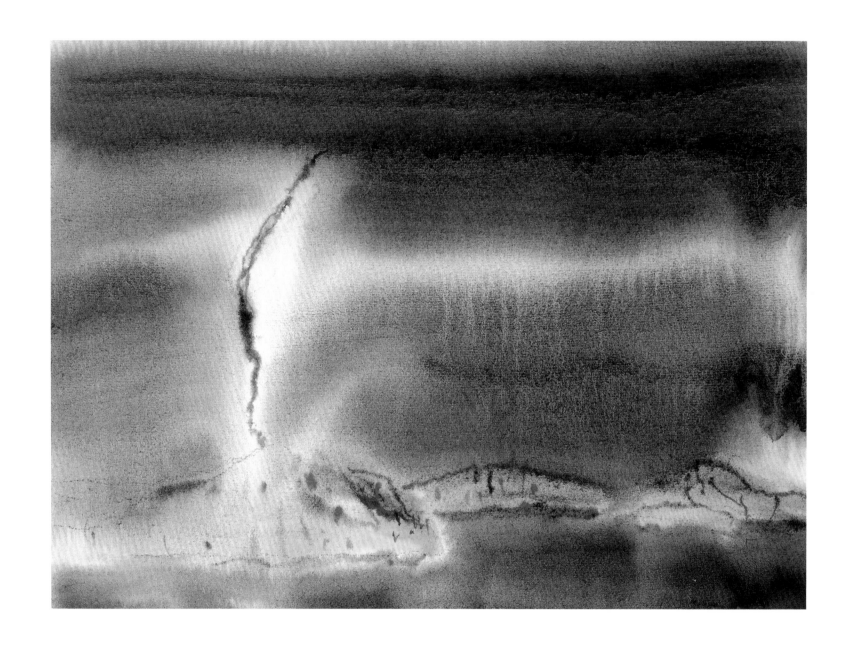

148 STORM OVER THE ISLANDS IV. Baptiste Lake, 10–17 November 1951. Watercolour over pencil on paper, 28 x 36.9. Art Gallery of Windsor, bequest of Frances Duncan Barwick.

206

149 LIGHTED STREETS II. A Toronto subject, painted at Baptiste Lake, November 1951. Watercolour over pencil on paper, 27.0 x 36.5. Edmonton Art Gallery, Alberta, gift from the Douglas M. Duncan Collection, 70.9.2.

Working on a larger picture started last spring or late winter "The Salesman" "Angels & Lipstick". Drawn in charcoal now, some changes in arrangement. The row of figures grouped. . . . Ungrouped there is a tendency to take each figure separately, almost to count them – slows up the movement across the picture. Changes in colour too, some subdued, some emphasised, again to speed up the movement.

Diary, 8 Nov 1952 [MFP]

150 TEMPTER WITH COSMETICS III. Baptiste Lake, 1952. Watercolour over pencil on paper, 54.9 x 75. Agnes Etherington Art Centre, Queen's University, Kingston, Chancellor Richardson Memorial Fund Purchase, 13-79.

Chronology

8 January 1882
David Brown Milne born near Borgoyne, Saugeen Township, Bruce County, the youngest of ten children.

1890–1903
Lives in Paisley, Ontario and c. 1900 works as a school teacher. Begins to take a commercial art course.

1903
Travels to New York.

1903–1906
Studies at Art Students League.

1906–11
Works as a commercial artist in New York.

1911
Begins making prints of New York City.

1912
Marries May "Patsy" Hegarty on 3 August 1912.

1913
Exhibits in Armory Show and at Montross Gallery. Has work reproduced in the *New York Times*.

1916
Moves to Boston Corners; begins correspondence with James Clarke.

1918–1919
Enlists in Canadian Army. Goes to England and France in 1919 and produces work for the War Records. Returns to Boston Corners in 1919.

1920–21
Lives in a small hut on Alander Mountain.

1921–23
At Dart's Lake and Mount Riga in the Adirondacks. Exhibits at Cornell. Begins colour drypoints.

1923–29
Summers at Big Moose Lake and, after 1924, winters at Lake Placid.

1923–1924
In Ottawa. Has large one-man show in Montreal.

1925
Stops painting watercolours.

1927
Gets a press for the drypoints.

1929
Returns to live in Canada. Summers in Temagami.

1930–33
A winter in Weston and later moves to Palgrave, Ontario.

1933
Moves to Six Mile Lake, his principal home until 1939.

1934
Makes a major sale to the Massey family and has first exhibit at Mellors Galleries in Toronto.

1935
Meets Douglas Duncan.

1938
Meets Kathleen "Wyb" Pavey (later Milne).
Douglas Duncan becomes his agent.

1939–1940
Moves to Toronto to live with Kathleen Milne.

1941–1952
Lives in Uxbridge but after 1948 does all
painting at Baptiste Lake, where he has built a
cabin.

1952
Moves to Bancroft, Ontario but soon suffers a
stroke.

1953
Suffers a second stroke and dies on 26 December.

ABBREVIATIONS

Massey Letter: David Milne to Vincent and Alice Massey, 20 August 1934, Massey Papers, Massey College. Quoted by permission of the Masters and Fellows of Massey College, in the University of Toronto, the owners of the letter, and of David Milne Jr, the owner of the copyright.

MFC: Milne Family Collection.
MFP: Milne Family Papers.
NAC: National Archives of Canada, Ottawa.
NGC: National Gallery of Canada, Ottawa.

MILNE AND HIS CONTEMPORARIES

1 Only a handful of Milnes are contained in public collections in the United States. Milne was included in an exhibition organized by the High Museum of Art in Atlanta, Georgia, in 1986, entitled *The Advent of Modernism: Post-Impressionism and North American Art, 1900–1918*, which has permitted his early work to be seen in a North American context.

2 David Milne, Autobiography, c. 1947, MFP.

3 John O'Brian, *David Milne and the Modern Tradition of Painting* (Toronto: Coach House Press, 1983), p 86.

4 See the Berkshire Museum's *Return to Arcadia: Nineteenth Century Berkshire County Landscape* (1990), for a history of artistic activity in that region.

5 According to Milne's autobiography, Boston Corners was not a chance discovery. He used contour maps to find a spot with hilly terrain dotted with lakes or ponds and near a railway so that he could send work to New York City. In addition to providing him with the painting material he needed, Boston Corners also afforded "ease and steadiness of life, and made few demands on the painter." It probably reminded him of the area in which he spent his boyhood – near Burgoyne in Bruce County, Ontario – and he often compared his chosen painting places with it: notably, when overseas as a war artist, and at Palgrave, Ontario, which he called "heaven located 35 miles northwest of Toronto," for it too provided the subject matter and the uninterrupted painting time he required.

6 *"Bright Garden": David Milne 1882–1953* (Toronto: Mira Godard Gallery, 18 October–5 November 1986), p 4. Wilkin cites John O'Brian's *David Milne and the Modern Tradition of Painting*, in which he asserts that Milne's art belies a contradiction between modernism and a more romantic approach to art.

7 In *World Art, Themes of Unity in Diversity: Acts of the XXVIth International Congress of the History of Art* (University Park and London: Pennsylvania State University Press, 1989), p 50.

8 Lora Carney has pointed out this influence in her essay in *David Milne: New York City Paintings 1910–1916* (Toronto: Mira Godard Gallery, 23 February–14 March 1984), unpaginated.

9 See Rosemarie L. Tovell, *Reflections in a Quiet Pool: The Prints of David Milne* (Ottawa: National Gallery of Canada, 1980), p 44, n 21. Tovell quotes from Milne's unpublished autobiography.

10 The drawings were shown in a special exhibition, *David Milne: Late New York Brush Drawings 1915–1916* (Toronto: Mira Godard Gallery, 6–31 March 1982).

11 Stieglitz married O'Keeffe in 1924, and carried on an extended correspondence with Dove and Marin for many years. The correspondence between Stieglitz and Dove, and Stieglitz and Marin, has been published in Ann Lee Morgan, ed., *Dear Stieglitz, Dear Dove* (Newark: University of Delaware Press, 1988); and Dorothy Norman, ed., *The Selected Writings of John Marin* (New York: Pellegrini and Cudahy, 1949).

12 Joyce Zemans, "David Milne 1911–1915," *Artscanada*, February-March 1973, p 73. As we know, Milne participated in the Armory Show as an uninvited exhibitor, represented by five works.

13 His friend James Clarke, who went on to become president of the New York advertising firm of Caulkins & Holden, helped relieve Milne of some of his financial burdens, as did Vincent and Alice Massey, and Douglas Duncan, in later years.

14 These observations are contained in the Massey Letter, 20 August 1934.

15 J.E.H. MacDonald to Milne, 27 July 1924, MFP.

16 Milne to H.O. McCurry, Assistant Director of the National Gallery of Canada, 28 March 1930, NGC. Milne imagined that they were aiming at a closely-knit exhibition to avoid the confusion characteristic of the OSA show, which he thought was a good idea. He anticipated seeing their show with some eagerness: "I am curious to see, too, whether their movement has had any effect on their color and shape or whether they have fallen into the weakness of the picturesque which marked the early art of Canada."

17 In his essay "Disunity as Unity: A Canadian Strategy," writer Robert Kroetsch discusses how Canadians have been uncertain about their heroes in literature. It is interesting to note his observation that "it is no accident that the hero of the Canadian story, often, is the artist." In *The Lovely Treachery of Words: Essays Selected and New* (Toronto: Oxford University Press, 1989), pp 28–31.

18 Donald W. Buchanan, "Roundabout on a Swing: Milne – An Artist in a Forest Hut," *Lethbridge Herald*, 2 November 1934; and "An Artist Who Lives in the Woods," *Saturday Night*, 1 December 1934. He also wrote the introductory essay for the catalogue of an *Exhibition of Paintings by David B. Milne* that was held at the Mellors Galleries, Toronto, 27 November–8 December 1934.

19 Kenneth Wells, "Log Cabin Artist Wins Contentment in North – Should One Envy Him His Lot?" *Telegram*, 29 September 1934; and "A Toast to a Painter and the Woods He Paints – The Story of a Man Who Had the Courage to Answer the Call of the Wilds," *Telegram*, undated clipping, probably November 1934.

20 Alan Jarvis, "Notes on Two Canadian Artists," *The Undergraduate* (University of Toronto), 1936, pp 35–36, and G. Campbell McInnes, "The World of Art," *Saturday Night*, 30 November 1935. McInnes explained the difference thus: "Whereas Thomson's decorative talent and his brilliance as a colorist make his intensity at once evident, Milne's intensity appears at first to be dissipated among his broken lines, his disjointed patches of

paint, and apparently empty bits of canvas. It is only after contemplation that … a highly concentrated essence … becomes apparent."

21 Blodwen Davies, *Paddle and Palette: The Story of Tom Thomson* (Toronto: Ryerson Press, 1930), pp 3, 33.

22 Draft letter from Milne to McCurry, April 1930, MFP.

23 Milne to McCurry, 1 April 1932, NGC. This letter was a response to the series of reproductions of Canadian paintings that the National Gallery began to produce in 1929.

24 Massey Papers, University of Toronto Archives. A large folder of press clippings concerning this exhibition was compiled by the Office of the High Commissioner for Canada (Vincent Massey), and contains 180 items. Presumably the fact that many of the regional newspapers received the same press releases accounts for the repetitious nature of the reviews. A sampling includes the following: "Artist Adventurers," *Paisley Sketch*, 15 October 1938; Eric Newton, "Canadian Art at the Tate: Paintings Inspired by Soil and Climate…," *Sunday Times*, 16 October 1938; Jan Gordon, "Canadian Art: Exhibition at Tate Gallery," *Observer*, 16 October 1938. Gordon wrote: "David B. Milne stands out with a style so individual that one would have to see more of his work to judge it fairly."

25 Eric Newton, "Canadian Art Through English Eyes," *Canadian Forum*, February 1939, pp 344–45.

26 Between *A Century of Canadian Art* and the Venice Biennale, Milne's work was included in all the major exhibitions of Canadian art shown abroad: the New York World's Fair (with the Canadian Group of Painters), 1939; *Canadian Painting*, Addison Gallery, Andover, Mass., 1942; *Canadian Art*, Yale University Art Gallery, 1944; *Painting in Canada: A Selective Historical Survey*, Albany Institute of History and Art, Albany, New York, 1946; *Forty Years of Canadian Painting: From Tom Thomson and the Group of Seven to the Present Day*, Museum of Fine Arts, Boston, 1949; *Canadian Painting*, National Gallery of Art, Washington, 1950; *Contemporary Canadian Graphic Arts*, University of Maine Art Gallery, Bangor, 1951.

27 G. Campbell McInnes, "Contemporary Canadian Artists No. 9: David B. Milne," *Canadian Forum*, October 1937, pp 238–39.

28 In his comments on some Canadian artists, Milne noted the influence of Gauguin and Van Gogh on Thomson and MacDonald in particular. Milne to McCurry, 1 April 1932, NGC Archives. See note 23. Van Gogh was extremely popular among some members of the Group of Seven around 1920: a petition was prepared by a number of members of the Arts and Letters Club in December 1920 to encourage the Art Gallery of Toronto to bring a show of his work up from New York. Among the signatories were Lawren S. Harris, Arthur Lismer, J.E.H. MacDonald, and Frank H. Johnston. It does not appear to have been presented to the Council of the Art Gallery, however, and was retained by Frederick S. Challener. It is now contained in the archives of the Arts and Letters Club. In any event, there is no record that the exhibition, probably the one that opened at the Montross Gallery, New York, in October 1920, was ever brought to the Art Gallery of Toronto.

29 See J. Russell Harper, *Painting in Canada: A History* (Toronto:

University of Toronto Press, 1966); Dennis Reid, *A Concise History of Canadian Painting* (Toronto: Oxford University Press, 1973); and Charles Hill, *Canadian Painting in the Thirties* (Ottawa: National Gallery of Canada, 1975).

30 Milne to McCurry, 7 January 1932, Correspondence with Artists, 7.1 M, NGC Archives. These comments were made about the last Group of Seven show held at the Art Gallery of Toronto in December 1931. Three works by FitzGerald were included: *Doc Snider's House*, *Farm Buildings*, and *Prairie Farm*.

31 Maxwell was an academic painter based in Montreal. Milne had read one of his reviews of an annual Royal Canadian Academy exhibition, probably that of the Fifty-Second Annual Exhibition in *The Journal, Royal Architectural Institute of Canada*, January 1932, pp 14–21.

32 Fragment of a typescript of letter to Buchanan, undated (mid-1930s), MFP.

33 Milne to Alice Massey, 13 September 1934, University of Toronto Archives. It is no. 12 on a list of pictures sent to the Masseys on 14 September 1934, MFP.

34 Milne to Clarke, 3 October 1932, MFP. All citations in this paragraph are from the same letter.

35 Milne to Clarke, 28 August 1935, MFP, quoted in Tovell, *Reflections in a Quiet Pool*, p 126.

36 Milne to Mrs Massey, 9 March 1939, MFP.

37 Throughout Milne's career, progress made in one medium often helped him solve formal problems in another: the war watercolours aided him in his use of oil paint in the early 1920s; and the drypoints helped in his use of oils a decade later at Palgrave. In a letter to fellow artist Carl Schaefer, Milne revealed, "My tendency is to run all the mediums together, oil, watercolour and etching, to work transparency … into oil, and opacity into watercolour and strangest of all, though etching is ordinarily the black and white medium, my etching depends more on hues and less on black and white than either of the other mediums. An interesting but dangerous tendency, you get into trying things that can't be done in the medium." 16 February 1938, MFP.

38 David Catton Rich, "John Marin – An Appreciation," unpublished manuscript, 1961, quoted in Sheldon Reich, *John Marin: A Stylistic Analysis and Catalogue Raisonné* (Tucson: The University of Arizona Press, 1970), pp 342–43.

39 Herbert J. Seligmann, ed., *Letters of John Marin* (New York: privately printed for An American Place, 1931), unpaginated. This is an excerpt from an article, "John Marin by Himself," first published in *Creative Art*, October, 1928.

40 Milne to Clarke, 13 November 1927, MFP, cited in Tovell, *Reflections in a Quiet Pool*, p 60, n. 13.

41 Massey Letter.

42 E.R. Hunter, *J.E.H. MacDonald: A Biography and Catalogue of His Work* (Toronto: Ryerson Press, 1940), p xii. In 1926 MacDonald prepared a lecture, "An Artist's View of Whitman." J.E.H. MacDonald Papers, NAC.

43 An autobiographical portrait written in 1930 and reprinted in Ann Lee Morgan, ed., *Dear Stieglitz, Dear Dove*, p 190.

44 Excerpt from "An Idea," written in 1927 and reprinted in Morgan, *Dear Stieglitz, Dear Dove*, p 146.

45 Milne to Graham McInnes, 16 February 1938, MFP.

46 Tovell, *Reflections in a Quiet Pool*, p 127.

47 Rough draft of comments on Group of Seven show, 1930, to Harry McCurry, April 1930, MFP.

48 Rough draft of letter, Milne to McCurry, 29 May–5 June 1932, MFP. It was this unity (an essential element in his own work, given that he wanted its esssence to be grasped at once) that Milne found uppermost in Morrice's art. He interpreted one of Morrice's statments, quoted by D.W. Buchanan in his 1937 monograph on Morrice, that "you should move ... from warm colours to cold colours, from neatness to disorder" (p 97), as the impressionist's creed of sacrificing the parts to the whole, that the artist should move from detail to unity (Milne to Buchanan, 19 January 1937, NGC). Milne remained an impressionist at heart; of all the paintings in an exhibition of "French Painting and Sculpture from the Kraushaar Galleries, New York" at the Art Gallery of Toronto in December 1929, Milne mentioned "two thrilling Pissarros" (*Market at Pontoise*, and *Landscape with Tree*) (Milne to McCurry, undated letter, NGC).

49 Draft letter to McCurry, Spring 1933 [?], MFP.

50 Milne to Clarke, 26 September 1931, MFP.

51 Milne to McCurry, 28 March 1930, NGC.

52 "Diagnoses Appeal of El Greco's Art: Mentality of Old Spanish Master Discussed by Bertram Brooker," *The Mail*, 1 March 1930.

DAVID MILNE'S NEW YORK

Thanks to David Milne Jr for his help with details of this article, for time spent showing me early Milne works in the Milne Family Collection, and for his generosity in sharing the vast amount of information on Milne's work collected over the years. – LSC

1 Clarke to Milne, 27 March 1918, MFP.

2 *Aliens* (Garden City, New York: Doubleday, Page & Co., 1918), pp 343–44. McFee stayed with friends in New Jersey across the Hudson from New York City for several months, writing this book, finishing the novel *Casuals of the Sea* (see note 19) and trying to sell both in the city before returning to sea. *Aliens* was first published in 1914 in London by Edward Arnold and in New York by Longmans, Green & Co. The second edition (released 27 February 1918) was slightly revised (see James T. Babb, *A Bibliography of the Writings of William McFee, with an Introduction and Notes by William McFee* [Garden City, New York: Doubleday, Doran & Co., 1931], pp 8, 17, 18). James Clarke commented in the letter cited above that "although he has rewritten it there still clings to it much of what I take to be the early influence of Conrad and Wells."

3 As a result of research conducted for this exhibition, a partial sketch of Amos Engle's life is now available. Engle was born in 1880 in Lumberton Township, New Jersey, to a Quaker farming family whose history in the area went back to pre-Revolutionary times. Once in New York, Engle and Milne not only worked together in their shop at 8 E. Forty-Second St (which became 20 E. Forty-Second St), but they also had pictures in the same society exhibitions in New York and Philadelphia, and at the Montross Gallery in New York. Engle went into military service for the United States during World War I, when Milne joined the Royal Canadian Army, and they never saw each other again, evidently having lost track of each other after exchanging a couple of postwar letters. Engle settled in San Francisco in 1920, established himself on Montgomery Street (in a section of the city known as an artists' quarter), and worked as a commercial artist. He married Fanny Goldsmith, a Russian-born San Francisco playwright and producer of marionette plays, in 1924. He made painting trips to Carmel, and exhibited at Stanford University and the San Francisco Art Association before his early death in 1926. (Ref. Peter Falk, ed., *Who was Who in American Art: Compiled from the Original Thirty-Four Volumes of American Art Annual* [Madison, Conn.: Sound View Press, 1985], p 188; E.M. Hughes, *Artists in California, 1786-1940* [San Francisco: Hughes Publishing Co., 1989], pp 145–46; D.F. Bostick and D. Castelhun, *Carmel at Work and Play* [Carmel: Seven Arts Press, 1925], p 58; State of New Jersey Birth Return dated 19 March 1880; State of California Marriage License, Local Reg. No. 2569 dated 2 June 1924; California State Board of Health Standard Certificate of Death, Local Reg. No. 1270, District 3801 dated 17 February 1926; and obituary for Engle, *San Francisco Chronicle*, 17 February 1926. p 14.)

I thank Ms Arlene Hess, Harrison Memorial Library, Carmel; and Ms Linda Zoeckler, Huntington Art Reference Library, San Marino, for their extensive efforts to help me find information about Amos Engle.

4 John O'Brian laid the groundwork for the study of Milne's formal sources in his excellent monograph *David Milne and the Modern Tradition of Painting* (Toronto: Coach House Press, 1983).

5 This date is used in such sources as Abraham H. Davidson, *Early American Modernist Painting 1910–1935* (New York: Harper and Row, 1981); William C. Agee, *Modern American Painting 1910–1940: Toward a New Perspective* (Houston: The Museum of Fine Arts, exhibition catalogue, 1977); and William Innes Homer, ed., *Avant-Garde: Painting and Sculpture in America 1910–1925* (Wilmington: Delaware Art Museum, 1975).

6 Robert Shackleton, *The Book of New York* (Philadelphia: The Penn Publishing Co., 1920, orig. 1917), p 68.

7 *King's Views of New York 1896–1915 and Brooklyn 1905*, compiled by Moses King, reissued with a new introduction by A.E. Santaniello (New York: Benjamin Blom, Inc., 1974), p 71.

8 William Wirt Mills, "New York City – The World's Commercial Centre," in *King's Views of New York 1896–1915 and Brooklyn 1905*.

9 Shackleton, *The Book of New York*, p 4.

10 Peter B. Hale, *Silver Cities: The Photography of American Urbanization, 1839–1915* (Philadelphia: Temple University Press, 1984), p 5.

11 *Skyscraperism: The Tall Office Building Artistically Considered, c. 1900–c. 1930*, the informal catalogue of an exhibition 1 February–15 March 1979 at the Wellesley College Museum, Wellesley, Massachusetts, has a good summary of New York skyscraper imagery by Weber, Walkowitz and other painters and by artist-photographers such as Stieglitz. "Skyscraperism" was a pejorative term coined by Frank Lloyd Wright.

12 Examples of these 1910 watercolours appear in *John Marin's New*

York (New York: Kennedy Galleries exhibition catalogue, 1981), plates 1 and 4–7.

According to Joyce Zemans, Milne's later Toronto agent Douglas Duncan stated that Milne met Marin at this time and even worked in Marin's style briefly (review of Milne exhibition at Marlborough Godard 16 November–9 December 1972, *Artscanada* 30:1 [February–March 1973], p 73).

13 Marin's famous foreword to his 1913 exhibition at Stieglitz's gallery is quoted in full in Ruth E. Fine, *John Marin* (Washington: National Gallery of Art exhibition catalogue, 1990), p 126.

14 *Skyscraperism*, pp 5 and 14. The painting, incorrectly titled at the time of the exhibition as *Woolworth Building*, is illustrated on p 5, and is in the Museum of Fine Arts, Boston.

15 William Innes Homer, *Alfred Stieglitz and the American Avant-Garde* (Boston: New York Graphic Society, 1977), pp 215–17. Plates 102 and 103 are examples of Walkowitz's "Improvisations of New York."

16 The few exceptions to this include a small group of etchings, 1911 or thereabouts, representing the Singer Building (the world's tallest building when completed in 1908), the Metropolitan Life Tower (the world's tallest the following year), the Brooklyn Bridge and other grand-scale monuments. However, Rosemarie Tovell, cataloguer of Milne's prints, believes these etchings had a commercial purpose and were less products of free will than his other New York City pictures. (See Tovell, *Reflections in a Quiet Pool: The Prints of David Milne* [Ottawa: National Gallery of Canada, 1980], p 17. The prints and their accompanying catalogue entries are on pp 22–33.).

17 Donelson Hoopes, *The American Impressionists* (New York: Watson-Gupthill Publications, 1972), p 72.

18 Anonymous, *American Art News* 4:10 (16 December 1905), p 1.

19 *Casuals of the Sea: The Voyage of a Soul* (Garden City, New York: Doubleday, Page & Co., 1923, first pub. 1917), p 381.

20 Pennell's autobiography, published the year before his death, was titled *The Adventures of an Illustrator, Mostly in Following His Authors in America and Europe* (Boston: Little, Brown and Co., 1925).

21 In a letter to his future wife, Milne called Pennell "about the best living etcher." 6 October [1909], Milne Papers, NAC.

22 *Pennell's New York Etchings: 90 Prints by Joseph Pennell*, selection and text by Edward Bryant (New York: Dover Publications, Inc. in cooperation with the Picker Art Gallery of Colgate Unversity, 1980), plate 6.

23 Pennell, in the *New York Times*, 24 April 1926, p 6; quoted in *Pennell's New York Etchings: 90 Prints*, p 95.

24 Pennell, "The Wonder of Work in the Northwest," *Harper's* 132 (March 1916): 591; quoted in *Pennell's New York Etchings: 90 Prints*, p xiv.

25 "The New Fifth Avenue," *Real Estate Record and Guide* 74 (17 December 1904): 1346; quoted in R.A.M. Stern, G. Gilmartin and J.M. Massengale, *New York 1900: Metropolitan Architecture and Urbanism 1890–1915* (New York: Rizzoli, 1983), p 195.

26 Anonymous, "The Point of View," *Scribner's* 7 (March 1890): 396; quoted in *New York 1900: Metropolitan Architecture and Urbanism 1890–1915*, p 20.

27 *John Sloan: New York City Etchings (1905–1949)*, ed. Helen Farr Sloan (New York: Dover Publications, Inc., 1978), plates 2, 4 and 5.

28 Ronald G. Pisano, *Idle Hours: Americans at Leisure 1865–1914* (Boston, Toronto and London: Little, Brown and Co., 1988), discusses Prendergast's paintings of leisure activities in their socio-historical context.

29 Nancy Mowll Mathews, *Maurice Prendergast* (Williamstown, Mass.: Williams College, 1990), pp 19–20.

30 Such a holiday was very typical for a New York artist. The *American Art News* of 6 May 1905 noted in an article called "For Summer Outings" (p 5) that for summer plans, "the mountains with their concomitants of peaceful valleys and beautiful clear lakes appeal most strongly, not only to the older painter, but to the young and to the thousands upon thousands of students who are beginning to transcribe upon canvas the lessons of Mother Nature." The article reports that while the Catskills were still visited, the Adirondacks (where Milne would settle for a time in 1916) were now accessible by the New York Central railroad and had become an even more popluar destination for artists.

31 Milne to Hegarty [April or May 1909], Milne Papers, NAC.

32 Griselda Pollock, *Vision and Difference: Femininity, Feminism and Histories of Art* (London and New York: Routledge, 1988), p 66.

33 "A Noted Impressionist: Atmospheric Notes from Town and Country by the Late Camille Pissaro [sic]," *New York Times*, 29 November 1903, p 13. The Monet painting in question was *View on the Seine*, according to another notice in *Hyde's Weekly Art News*, Fourth Issue, Second Year, week ending 28 November 1903, p 1.

BOSTON CORNERS

1 Massey Letter, 20 August 1934.

2 Ibid.

3 Ibid.

4 Ibid. As we will see, artistically the move was far from a tragedy. Perhaps Milne meant an economic tragedy.

5 Boston Corners Autobiography, February–March 1947, MFP.

6 Ibid.

7 Ibid.

8 Ibid.

9 Ibid.

10 Ibid.

11 Although identified as Bishop's Pond by Douglas Duncan, the subject is in fact the Kelly Ore Bed.

12 John O'Brian, *David Milne and the Modern Tradition of Painting* (Toronto: Coach House Press, 1983), p 86.

13 Dazzle spots were areas of white which contrasted violently with dark areas in a composition and thus enlivened it.

14 Boston Corners Autobiography, MFP.

15 Ibid.

16 Ibid.

17 He wrote to the Masseys that he had enlisted in February 1918 but it seems unlikely that he would have been able to conclude

his affairs in Boston Corners in less than a month.

18 War Records Autobiography, MFP.
19 Ibid.
20 Milne to James Clarke, 6 December 1918, Milne Papers, NAC. Letters of 6 and 7 December 1918 (Milne Papers, NAC) ask Clarke to canvas support and gather up work for shipment to London.
21 War Records Autobiography, MFP.
22 Ibid.
23 A.Y. Jackson, *A Painter's Country* (Toronto: Clarke, Irwin and Company, 1976), p 46.
24 Ibid.
25 For a full account of the establishment and operation of the Canadian War Records or more correctly the Canadian War Memorials Fund, see Maria Tippett, *Art at the Service of War: Canada, Art, and the Great War* (Toronto: University of Toronto Press, 1984).
26 War Records Autobiography.
27 Ibid.
28 Ibid.
29 Ibid.
30 Ibid.
31 Milne to Clarke, 9 April 1919, Milne Papers, NAC.
32 Massey Letter.
33 Ibid.
34 A total of 112 war works remain (some are double sheets) of which 107 are part of the War Records collection now in the NGC.
35 Milne to Clarke, 11 February 1919, Milne Papers, NAC.
36 Anonymous, *Canadian Daily Record*, February 18, 1919.
37 Milne to Clarke, 9 April 1919, Milne Papers, NAC.
38 Massey Letter.
39 Ibid.
40 War Records Autobiography, MFP.
41 The letters of 24, 26 June and 7, 8 July 1919 (Milne Papers, NAC) in particular.
42 Massey Letter.
43 War Records Autobiography, MFP.
44 Milne to Clarke, 17 December 1919, Milne Papers, NAC.
45 Rosemarie Tovell, *Reflections in a Quiet Pool: The Prints of David Milne* (Ottawa: National Gallery of Canada, 1980), p 1.
46 Boston Corners Painting Notes, No. 15, 30 December 1919, Milne Papers, NAC.
47 Milne to James Clarke, 9 January 1920, Milne Papers, NAC.
48 Boston Corners Painting Notes, No. 54, 20 February 1920, Milne Papers, NAC.
49 Boston Corners Painting Notes, No. 115, 24 August 1920, Milne Papers, NAC.
50 Boston Corners Painting Notes, No. 118, 27 August 1920, Milne Papers, NAC.
51 Boston Corners Autobiography, MFP.
52 For a full account of this time see, David Milne, "David Milne: His Journal and Letters of 1920 and 1921: A Document of Survival," *Artscanada*, August 1973, pp 15–55.

CREATIVE COURAGE

All quotations from Milne's letters to Clarke are taken from typescripts included in the MFP. The original handwritten letters are held by the NAC, Ottawa. The Massey Letter of 1934 is likewise quoted from typescript. The original letter can be found at the archives of Massey College, University of Toronto. – MB
   Unless otherwise noted, the author is David Milne.

1   Draft letter to Spencer Kellogg, 29 December [?] 1930, MFP.
2   Letter to James Clarke from Dart's Camp, 28 June 1921, MFP.
3   Milne diary c. spring 1923, MFP.
4   Massey Letter, 20 August 1934. Unless otherwise noted, all following quotations are from this letter of 1934.
5   Letter to Clarke from Bramshott, England, 9 April 1919, MFP.
6   Letter to Clarke from Seaford and London, England, 7, 15 May 1919, MFP.
7   Massey Letter.
8   Boston Corners Painting Notes, 7 January 1920, MFP.
9   All quotations on building the cabin are from a letter to Clarke, from Boston Corners, 30 September 1920, MFP.
10 Letter to Clarke from Kinmel Park Camp, 1, 6, 11 October 1918, MFP.
11 Autobiography, c. 1947, Alander, p 104, MFP.
12 Massey Letter.
13 Henry David Thoreau, *Walden*, ed. J. Lyndon Shanley, Princeton University Press, Princeton, New Jersey, 1971, p 15.
14 All quotations regarding *Drift on the Stump* come from a letter to Clarke from the Alander cabin, 11 February 1921, MFP.
15 Comment on the *Black Waterfall* and that following are from a letter to Clarke from the Alander cabin, early April 1921, MFP.
16 Letter to Mrs Alice Massey, 13 September 1934, MFP. The original of this letter is in the University of Toronto Archives.
17 Autobiography, c. 1947, Alander, p 116, MFP.
18 Letter to Clarke from Mt Riga, 25 May 1921, MFP.
19 Letter to Clarke from Palgrave, 15 October 1930, MFP.
20 Autobiography, c. 1947, Dart's Lake, MFP.
21 Massey Letter.
22 Letter to Clarke from Dart's Camp, 28 June 1921, MFP.
23 Letter to Clarke from Mt Riga, 14 February 1922, MFP.
24 Letter to Clarke from Mt Riga [?], 22 November 1922, MFP.
25 All quotations regarding Monet are from "Art. Monet," undated, MFP.
26 All comments on etching at Mt Riga are from the autobiography, c. 1947, Mt Riga, MFP.
27 Letter to Clarke from Ottawa, c. 23 October 1923, MFP.
28 Autobiography, c. 1947, Ottawa, p 5, MFP.
29 "Art General Outline," c. 1923, MFP.
30 Massey Letter.
31 Letter to Clarke from Big Moose, 23 August 1925, MFP.
32 Letter to Clarke from Lake Placid, 17, 20, 27 January 1925, MFP.
33 Letter to Clarke from Big Moose, 23 June 1925, MFP.
34 Letter to Clarke from Big Moose, 25 November 1925, MFP.
35 Letter to Clarke from Big Moose, 4 May 1926, MFP.

36 Letter to Clarke from Big Moose, 3 June 1926, MFP.

37 Letter to Clarke, last Sunday in September, 1926, MFP.

38 Lake Placid Diary, undated, MFP.

39 Letter to Clarke from Big Moose, late June, early [6, 11, 16] July 1926, MFP.

40 Ibid.

41 Letter to Clarke from Big Moose, late [27] August, 4, 14, 26, September 1926, MFP.

42 Letter to Clarke, 7 January 1927, MFP.

43 The close interrelationships of etching and painting have been admirably and definitively examined by Rosemarie Tovell in *David Milne: Painting Place*, from the series Masterpieces in the National Gallery of Canada (Ottawa: National Gallery of Canada, 1976); and *Reflections in a Quiet Pool: The Prints of David Milne* (Ottawa: National Gallery of Canada, 1980). Thus, the subject will not be discussed in depth in this essay.

44 Massey Letter.

45 Letter to Clarke from Lake Placid, 21, 23, 24, January 1929, MFP.

46 All comments are quoted or paraphrased from a letter to Clarke from Temagami, 21 June and later June 1929, MFP.

47 "Feeling in Painting," undated manuscript, MFP. (Published in modified form in 1948).

48 Massey Letter.

49 Letter to Clarke from Palgrave, 26 September 1931, MFP.

50 Ibid.

51 Letter to Maulsby Kimball from Palgrave, 9 March 1931, MFP.

52 Letter to Clarke from Alander, 21 April 1921, MFP.

53 Letter to Clarke, 13 November 1927, MFP.

54 *Twanging a Lyre*, undated manuscript, MFP.

55 Letter to Clarke from Palgrave, 10–26 April 1932, MFP.

56 Letter to Clarke from Palgrave, 3 October 1932, MFP.

57 Letter to Clarke from Big Moose, c. 13 November 1927, MFP.

58 It is interesting to note that Milne criticized the work of the Group of Seven for its reliance on subject matter to depict the Canadian experience. Nonetheless, of that generation "Tom Thomson still stands as *the* Canadian painter, harsh, brilliant, brittle, uncouth, not only most Canadian but most creative." Milne to H.O. McCurry, Assistant Director of the NGC, regarding the 1930 Group of Seven exhibition. The original of the letter is in the National Gallery Archives.

59 Letter to Clarke from Palgrave, 3 October 1932, MFP.

60 Letter to Clarke from Big Moose, 26 July 1925, MFP.

61 Answer to a questionnaire, 1942, MFP.

62 Luke 11:41–42

63 Answer to a questionnaire, 1942, MFP.

MILNE AND ABSTRACTION

1 "Ressemblant" in the original.

2 D. Buchanan, "Roundabout on a Swing: Milne – An Artist in a Forest Hut," *Lethbridge Herald*, 2 November 1934. Passage reprinted without any change in the preface to the catalogue of Milne's exhibition at the Mellors Galleries, Toronto, 27 November–8 December 1934.

3 D. Buchanan, "An Artist Who Lives in the Woods," *Saturday Night*, 50:4 (1 December 1934), p 2.

4 Massey Letter. We know that Milne's argument bore fruit, as the Masseys were to acquire about 300 pictures and arrange for Milne to have the services of Mellors Galleries in the years to come.

5 Milne to James Clarke, 11 June 1933, Milne Papers, NAC.

6 Diary, 26 April 1940, quoted in Rosemarie L. Tovell, *Reflections in a Quiet Pool: The Prints of David Milne* (Ottawa: National Gallery of Canada, 1980), p 118.

7 For this source see John O'Brian, *David Milne and the Modern Tradition in Painting* (Toronto: Coach House Press, 1983), p 89.

8 Again in the letter to the Masseys.

9 Anonymous article published in *La Presse* (Montreal), 23 March 1935; in the Milne file at the National Gallery of Canada.

10 Extract from an article entitled: "A Fauve: David B. Milne," published in an unidentified magazine which has been dated March 1935 but alludes to his exhibition at Scott's, which continued to 1 April 1935. Milne file, NGC.

11 Milne to H.O. McCurry, 17 March 1931, NGC.

12 Milne to Clarke, end of October 1933, Milne Papers, NAC.

13 See J. O'Brian, op. cit., pp 72–73.

14 Milne illustrates his idea at this point by two small sketches representing a roof gable, simply drawn in one case, and in the other with the shadow modelled in.

15 Milne to Clarke, 12 January 1931, Milne Papers, NAC.

16 See Rosemarie L. Tovell, op. cit., pp 146–47, who gives the letter of 12 January 1931 among the references for this etching.

17 Milne to Clarke, 3 September 1933, NAC.

18 Tovell, p 127, referring to a draft letter from Milne to Clarke, dated 2 April 1933, from Palgrave; Massey Family Papers, NAC.

THE LATE WORK OF DAVID MILNE

1 David Milne, diary, 26 April, 1940, MFP.

2 Milne to Douglas Duncan, 6 February 1938, MFP.

3 Milne to Alice Massey, 1 July 1937, Massey Family Papers, NAC.

4 Milne to James Clarke, 8 October 1933, Milne Papers, NAC.

5 Lora Senechal Carney, "David Milne: 'Subject Pictures'," *The Journal of Canadian Art History* 10:2 (1987), p 112. Many of the arguments presented here are indebted to Carney.

6 Milne to Maulsby Kimball, 25 December 1938, Milne Papers, NAC.

7 Milne to Carl Schaefer, 30 December 1938, Schaefer Papers, NAC.

8 Ibid.

9 Ibid.

10 Milne to Alan Jarvis, 15, 22, 30 January 1939, Jarvis Papers, NGC, copy in the MFP.

11 Ibid.

12 The three uncancelled versions are NGC (included here); the McMichael Canadian Art Collection (the version that was given to Miss Cowan); and Milne Family Collection. The two cancelled versions are also in the Milne Family Collection.

13 Milne to Alice Massey, 9 March 1939, Massey Family Papers, NAC.

14 Milne to Clarke, 10, 14 February 1941, Milne Papers, NAC.

15 Milne to Jarvis, 15, 22, 30 January 1939, Jarvis Papers, NGC.

16 An account of this period can be found in David Milne Jr, *David Milne: The Toronto Year 1939–1940* (Toronto: Marlborough Godard, 1976).

17 Ibid., p 5.

18 The work was listed in 1941 as *Mars Over Bay Street* but this is likely an error.

19 *David Milne: The Toronto Year*, p 6.

20 Tovell, *Reflections in a Quiet Pool: The Prints of David Milne* (Ottawa: National Gallery of Canada, 1980), p 175.

21 Milne to Schaefer, 13, 14 January 1941, Schaefer Papers, NAC.

22 Ibid.

23 Milne as quoted by Duncan in Tovell, op. cit., p 193.

24 Tovell, loc. cit.

25 Tovell, p 77.

26 Tovell, p 78.

27 Milne to James Clarke, 10 December 1941, Milne Papers, NAC.

28 John O'Brian has examined this "radical redirection" in Milne's work at length, *David Milne and the Modern Tradition of Painting* (Toronto: Coach House Press, 1983), pp 118–28.

29 O'Brian, p 127.

30 Carney, op. cit., p 115.

31 Both Carney and O'Brian have commented on Milne's religious beliefs.

32 Milne to Alan Jarvis, undated, Jarvis Papers, NGC, copy in the MFP.

33 Tovell, op. cit., p 187.

34 Ibid.

35 David Milne Jr has noted that Milne was, initially, "almost violent" in his approach to the Baptiste Lake landscape. *David Milne at Baptiste Lake* (Belleville: Belleville Public Library, 1984), p 11.

36 Milne diary, 16, 17 November 1951, MFP.

37 David Milne Jr, *David Milne at Baptiste Lake*, p 15.

38 Identified as such by David Milne Jr, *David Milne at Baptiste Lake*, p 20.

39 Milne Diary, 10 March 1952, MFP.

40 David Milne, "Feeling in Painting," *Here and Now* 1 (May 1948), p 57.

41 Milne to Spencer Kellogg, draft letter, 29 December [?], 1930, Milne Papers, NAC.

Notes to the Plates

1 Signed, lower left: David Milne June 1936. Inscription: 28 / Summer Colours.

2 Signed, lower left: David Milne / 1930.

3 Signed, middle right: (MR) DAVID B MILNE / FEB 9 1921.

4 Signed, upper right and lower left: David Milne.

5 Signed, lower right: David B Milne.

6 Signed, lower right: David B Milne.

7 Signed, upper right: David B. Milne.

8 Dated, lower left: July 24 15.

9 Dated, lower left: May 1 15.

10 Signed, upper left: DAVID B MILNE / DART'S CAMP / SEPT 9 /21. Inscribed (verso): David Milne: Rustic Washroom / Sept. 9, 1921 / (Dart's Camp, Adirondacks).

11 Signed, upper left: David Milne 1938.

12 Signed, middle left: David Milne / 1937.

13 Signed, lower right: David Milne 1936.

14 Signed, lower left: David B. Milne 1930.

15 Not signed or dated.

16 Signed in 1946, lower left: Milne.

17 Not signed or dated.

18 Signed in 1946, lower left: MILNE.

19 Signed, lower middle right: David B Milne – 15 [or 16]. Cancelled inscription: #19 Black Hills.

20 Signed, lower left: David B Milne '15.

21 Signed, lower right: David B. Milne.

22 Signed in 1946, upper right: David Milne.

23 Not signed or dated.

24 Tovell 19, only state.

25 Signed, lower right: David B. Milne.

26 Signed, lower left: David B. Milne. *Billboards* may have been exhibited at the Armory Show, New York, as *Columbus Circle* (cat. no. 796).

27 Signed in 1946, upper right: David Milne.

28 Signed, lower left: David B. Milne. Inscribed: White Matrix // #11.

29 Not signed or dated.

30 Not signed or dated.

31 Not signed or dated. Inscribed: Wood Interior #4.

32 Not signed or dated. Inscribed: Palisades Trees.

33 Signed in 1946, upper left: MILNE.

34 Dated, lower left: May 31–16. Inscribed: Green Masses 54.

35 Signed, lower left: Sept. 7.17 / D.B. Milne. Verso: *Row of Trees, Bisected*, 14 May 1916. Cancelled inscription: Catskills #3 / Last.

36 Dated, lower right: Sept 8–17.

37 Signed, middle right: David B Milne / Oct 21 '17.

38 Signed, lower middle: David B Milne Nov 10–17. Inscribed: Afternoon Light.

39 Signed, lower right: DAVID B MILNE / THE TWINS CRATER / JUNE 28 19. Inscribed: "THE TWINS" CRATER / VIMY RIDGE.

40 Signed, upper middle right: DAVID B MILNE / THELUS JUNE 30 19. Inscribed: SHATTERED / IMAGES IN THELUS CEMETERY.

41 Signed, lower left: DAVID B MILNE / MAPLE COPSE – ZILLE-

BEKE / AUG 14.19. Inscribed: MAPLE COPSE AND OBSERVATORY RIDGE / FROM DORMY HOUSE.

42 Signed, lower right: DAVID B. MILNE / AUG 24 '20.

43 Signed, middle left: DAVID B. MILNE / AUG 27 '20.

44 Signed in 1946, lower left: David Milne.

45 Signed, lower right: David B Milne. Fortunately, Clarke did not comply with Milne's request to send *Relaxation* to London. All fifteen of the pictures he did send in support of Milne's application for a position with the Canadian War Records were subsequently lost.

46 Signed, lower left: David B. Milne / Oct 4.16. Verso: *Burst of Trees II*, 1916. Inscribed: Bishops Pond. The upper left corner is repainted on a paper overlay. The picture has been exhibited in the past as *Reflections*.

47 Signed in 1946, lower middle: David Milne.

48 Signed, lower right: David B Milne Nov 1–17. Inscribed: Reflected Forms 100.

49 Signed in 1946, upper left: David Milne.

50 Not signed or dated.

51 Signed, lower right: DAVID B MILNE / RIPON CAMP / FEB 27.19.

52 Signed, upper left: DAVID B MILNE / BRAMSHOTT / APRIL 14–19. Inscribed: The Catholic Women's League / Hut. Bramshott Camp.

53 Signed on top sheet, upper left: DAVID B MILNE / ARRAS JULY 30 19. The title is also inscribed on the back of each sheet. The sheets were executed independently and can be viewed separately as complete works, as well as together.

54 Signed, lower right: DEC 21 19 / DAVID B MILNE 9.

55 Signed, lower right: 15 / DAVID B MILNE DEC 30.

56 Signed, lower middle: DAVID B. MILNE / FEB 20 '20.

57 Signed, lower right: DAVID B MILNE / AUG 27 '20.

58 Signed, lower right: DAVID B MILNE / MARCH 28 '21.

59 Signed in 1946, middle left: David / Milne. The final version of *Black Waterfall*, on 46 x 56 cm (18 x 22 inch) canvas, is probably a repainting of the 51 x 61 cm (20 x 24 inch) canvas described in Milne's letter to Clark.

60 Tovell 60, two states. State shown: II/II.

61 Signed, lower right: DAVID B MILNE FEB 10 1921.

62 Signed, upper right: DAVID B MILNE / MAY 15 '21.

63 Signed, upper right: DAVID B MILNE / DART'S LAKE SEPT 19 '21 / M.R. 22.

64 Signed, upper left: DAVID B MILNE / OTTAWA NOV 7.

65 Signed, upper right: DAVID B MILNE DEC. 1923.

66 Not signed or dated. Verso: *Old R.C.M.P. Barracks I*, plate 67.

67 Signed, upper left: DAVID B MILNE OTTAWA JAN 8 1924. Verso: *Porch at Night*, plate 66.

68 Signed, lower middle: DAVID MILNE 1925. This work was commissioned in 1925 by Caulkins & Holden, a New York advertising firm of which James Clark later became president.

69 Signed, upper right: David Milne 1931.

70 Signed, lower right: David Milne 1931.

71 Signed, upper left: David Milne 1931.

72 Not signed or dated.

73 Signed, lower right: DAVID B MILNE DART'S CAMP / OCT 4

218

'21. There is a faint pencil sketch of the main lodge in the lower centre of the picture.

74 Tovell 56, three states. State shown: III/III.

75 Signed, upper right: DAVID B MILNE FEB '23.

76 Not signed or dated.

77 Signed, upper right: David Milne Sept 4 1923.

78 Signed in 1946, lower right: David Milne. A third and final version of this subject was painted at Big Moose in August 1925.

79 Not signed or dated.

80 Not signed or dated. Verso: a pencil sketch of snow-covered evergreens.

81 Not signed or dated.

82 Signed, possibly in 1936, upper left: David Milne. Inscribed: 2 / Clouds below the Mountain Tops // Purple Red Woods w Bl detail / Red Barns & Black w purple detail / Brown & Black H / Gray Black & O Red H / Green & Black School / Purple near hills / Blue far hills.

83 Signed, lower left: David Milne.

84 Signed, lower right: DAVID B MILNE OCT 1926–JAN 1928.

85 Tovell 61, seven states. State shown: VII/VII.

86 Not signed or dated.

87 Signed, upper left: David Milne 1931.

88 Signed, upper left: David Milne 1931.

89 Signed, lower right: David Milne 1936. Inscribed: 27 / Lightning.

90 Not signed or dated.

91 Signed in 1946, lower left: Milne.

92 Signed, lower right: David Milne '39.

93 Not signed or dated.

94 Not signed or dated. Inscribed, possibly by the artist: Silver.

95 Signed, lower right: David B Milne 1929.

96 Not signed or dated.

97 Signed, possibly later, lower right: David Milne.

98 Signed, upper right: David B Milne / 1930.

99 Signed, upper right: David Milne 1931.

100 Signed, upper right: David Milne 1933.

101 Signed, upper left: David Milne 1935. Inscribed on the upper edge: D Sugar Bush.

102 Signed, upper left: David Milne 1935.

103 Signed, upper right: DAVID MILNE MARCH 1936. Inscribed: 35 / The Big Dipper.

104 Not signed or dated. Inscribed: 37 / Yellow Coat.

105 Signed, lower left: David Milne 1936. Inscribed: 12 / Bare Rock Begins to Show.

106 Signed, lower right: David Milne.

107 Tovell 74, two states. State show: II/II.

108 Signed, upper left: David Milne 1937. Inscribed: 28 / New Shelf / David Milne.

109 Not signed or dated.

110 Tovell 80, four states. State shown: IV/IV.

111 Not signed or dated.

112 Tovell 78, five states. State shown: V/V.

113 Not signed or dated.

114 Not signed or dated. Inscribed: Rites of Autumn.

115 Not signed or dated.

116 Not signed or dated.

117 Not signed or dated.

118 Not signed or dated.

119 Not signed or dated.

120 Signed, lower middle: David Milne / 1937. Inscribed: RED NASTURTIUMS / DAVID MILNE.

121 Signed, lower right: David Milne 1937. Inscribed: 30 / PIC-TURE ON THE BLACKBOARD.

122 Not signed or dated.

123 Signed, lower right: David Milne 1939.

124 Signed, upper right: David Milne 1940.

125 Signed in 1946, lower right: David Milne.

126 Not signed or dated.

127 Signed, lower right: David Milne 1940. Inscribed: Muddy Don.

128 Not signed or dated.

129 Dated, lower right: August 1941.

130 Dated, lower middle: Jan 1942.

131 Not signed or dated.

132 Not signed or dated. Inscribed: Eatons – College St.

133 Not signed or dated. Inscribed: "King and Queen with Jokers".

134 Not signed or dated. Verso: vertical version of *Palgrave 1932–1944*.

135 Not signed or dated.

136 Signed in 1946, upper left: David Milne.

137 Dated, upper right: JUNE 1945.

138 Not signed or dated.

139 Not signed or dated.

140 Signed, lower right: David Milne JUNE '46.

141 Not signed or dated.

142 Not signed or dated.

143 Not signed or dated.

144 Not signed or dated.

145 Not signed or dated.

146 Not signed or dated.

147 Not signed or dated.

148 Not signed or dated.

149 Not signed or dated.

150 Not signed or dated.

220

Index

The Index lists only persons and paintings. Bold figures are plate numbers; roman figures are page numbers.

Across from the Garage   113
Across the Lake   **73**, **74**, 103
Across the Still Lake   **13**, 33
Afternoon Light   **38**
Alcove   **29**
Ascension   **134**, **135**, 167

Bare Rock Begins to Show   **105**
Battery Park   **39**
Beaverbrook, William Maxwell Aitken, Lord   17, 71
Bell, Clive   30, 35, 132
Bialostocki, Jan   21–22
Big Dipper   **103**
Billboard   **17**, 43
Billboards   **26**, 13
Bishop's Pond   **46**, 64
Bishop's Pond in Sunlight   133
Black   **6**, 13, 43
Black Cabinet   **76**
Black Reflections   **48**, 64
Black Waterfall   **59**, 97, 101
Blind Road   **14**, 33
Blossom Pickers   **23**
Blue-Green, Black-Green   13
Borduas, Paul-Emile   19
Boston Corners   **50**, 67
Botanical Museum, Bronx Park   43, 63
Boulder   **44**, 64
Brooker, Bertram   29, 33–35
Brush Fire   **118**
Buchanan, Donald   19, 26, 29, 131, 135

Campfire in Winter   **142**
Candy Box   27
Carnival Dress   **78**, 108
Carr, Emily   27, 29
Cathedral, Arras   **53**, 73
Catholic Women's League Hut, Bramshott Camp   **52**, 72
Cézanne, Paul   18, 29, 35, 115, 141
Chestnut and Laurel   **18**, 64
Chocolates and Flowers   **125**, 162

Clarke, James   11, 12, 17, 63, 72, 73, 75, 99, 100, 103, 132, 139, 163
Classen Point Road   12
Clouds at the Horizon   136
Clouds Below the Mountain Tops   **82**
Columbus Circle   13
Columbus Monument   27
Comfort, Charles   33, 34
Contours and Elms   **98**
Cross Chute   **11**, 27, 30, 161

Davies, Arthur   12
Dominion Square   **78**
Dove, Arthur   23, 31, 32
Dow, Arthur Wesley   23
Drift on the Stump   **61**, 101
Duncan, Douglas   19, 26, 160, 162
Dutchman's Breeches   **126**

E.B. Eddy Mill, Hull, Quebec   **65**
Earth, Sky and Water   **138**, **139**
Eatons, College Street   **132**
Emerson, Ralph Waldo   141
Engle, Amos   37, 40
Exhibition of Little Pictures catalogue, quoted   4, 140

Fairley, Barker   160
Fifth Avenue from the Steps of the New York Public Library   **24**
First Snow   **109**
FitzGerald, LeMoine   29, 33
Five Trees and Dome   **8**
Flowers and Easel   **97**, 111
Framed Etching   **88**, 114
From the Cabin Door   **143**
From the Painting House   75

Gateleg Table   **62**, 101
Gauguin, Paul   27, 29
Gentle Snowfall   **55**, 75
Glass Candlestick   **140**
Goodbye to a Teacher   **122**, 161, 162, 167, 180
Grand Concourse, Bronx   **33**
Gray, Brown and Black   **20**, 63

Greco, El   29, 35
Green Masses   **34**
Grey Billboards   **25**
Group of Seven   25, 26, 27, 29, 32
Gulls and Lighthouse   **113**
Gully   **56**, 79

Harper, J. Russell   29
Harris, Lawren   33, 35
Hassam, Childe   17, 39, 41
Haystack   **75**, 103
Henri, Robert   12, 37–38
Hillside, Berkshires   **49**, 67
Hopper, Edward   12
House of Commons   **64**, 105–108
Hudson from Weehawken   **7**, 13

Interior of the Tea House   **77**

Jackson, A.Y.   29, 33, 34, 71, 160
Jarvis, Alan   19–20, 26, 160, 161
Jerome Avenue, The Bronx   **19**
Joe Lee's Hill   **34**, 63

King, Queen and Jokers   **133**, 163
Kitchen Chimney   **71**, 114
Konody, P.G.   17, 71, 72

Lake   **118**, 169
Lanterns and Snowshoes   **77**
Large Tree   **9**, 23, 63
Lighted Streets   **149**, 169, 202
Lightning   **89**
Lilies   **30**
Lilies from the Bush   **88**
Lismer, Arthur   71, 160

McCarthy, Pearl   19, 160
MacDonald, J.E.H.   18, 25, 26, 32
McFee, William   37, 38, 39–40
McInnes, Graham   19, 26, 27
Main Street   **110**
Maple Blooms on Hiram's Farm   **100**
Maple Copse and Observatory Ridge from Dormy House   **41**, 75

Marin, John   23, 30, 31–32, 37, 38, 39, 40
Massey, Alice & Vincent   11, 18–19, 25
    letter to   11, 17, 30, 32, 55, 100–101, 113, 114, 131, 132, 133
Matisse, Henri   12, 26, 29, 35, 136–9
Maxwell, W.S.   29
Midjo, Christian   17
Milne, David Jr   20, 195
Milne, Kathleen Pavey   19, 20, 162, 173, 195
Milne, Patsy Hegarty   15, 37, 68, 69, 82, 100, 103, 111, 113
Mondrian, Piet   135
Monet, Claude   29, 33, 45, 103, 149
Monkey and Orange Lilies   **136**
Morrice, J.W.   20, 29, 33, 35, 71
Mountains   **35**
Muddy Don   **127**

New Shelf   **108**, 32
Ninth Avenue El   **15**
Noah and the Ark and Mt Ararat   **130**, 167, 187

O'Brian, John   9, 21, 64, 136
O'Keefe, Georgia   23
Oil Can   **141**
Old R.C.M.P. Barracks   **67**
Ollie Matson's House Is Just a Square Red Cloud   **99**, 113, 141
Ollie Matson's House in Snow   **141**
Open Stream   **3**
Outlet of the Pond   **83**, **85**, 139
Outlet of the Pond, Morning   **84**, 110

Painting Place   **2**, 25, 27, 110
Palisades Trees   **32**, 64
Pansies and Yellow Box   **137**
Pellan, Alfred   27
Pennell, Joseph   12, 40, 41
Picture on the Blackboard   **121**, 161
Piero di Cosimo   29
Pink Reflections, Bishop's Pond   **42**, 79
Pollock, Griselda   45
Pool and Birches   **37**
Pool, Contours   **57**, 79

Porch at Night **66**
Porch of Summer Camp **10**, 25
Prendergast, Maurice 12, 13, 38, 43, 56
Prospect Shaft **86**, 133

Queen's Hotel, Palgrave **87**, 113, 136
Quiet River **144**

R.I.P. **115**
Red **5**, 12, 13, 43
Red Church **93**
Red Nasturtiums **120**, 32, 161
Reflected Forms **48**, 64
Reflections **47**
Relaxation **45**, 64
Ripon High Street **51**, 72
Rites of Autumn **114**
Roberts, Goodridge 27, 71

Saint **131**, 167
St Michael's Cathedral **124**, 162, 163
Scaffolding **116**, 167
Schaefer, Carl 163
Serenity **69**, 113
Shattered Images in Thelus Cemetery **40**, 75
Sheeler, Charles 12
Shelter at Night **117**, 169
Shore Line **106**
Shore Line with Stumps **107**
Ski-Jump Hills with Radiating Clouds **80**
Ski-Jump, Lake Placid **79**
Snow in Bethlehem **129**, 163, 167, 187
Sparkle of Glass **94**
Spider Bridge **119**, 169
Spuyten Duyvil **21**
Stars over Bay Street **90, 91**, 162, 169
Stars over Bay Street, Dark Version **128**
Stieglitz, Alfred 21, 23, 37, 45
Still Water **111**, 163
Still Water and Fish **112**, 163
Storm over the Islands **145, 146, 147, 148**, 169, 202
Sugar Bush **101**
Summer Colors **1**
Sunburst over the Catskills **36**, 65

Tempter with Cosmetics **150**, 169
Thomson, Tom 20, 26–27, 31
Thoreau, Henry David 21, 29, 32, 79, 100, 101, 141
Tin Basin, Flowers in a Prospector's Cabin **95**, 111
Tovell, Rosemarie 9, 75, 141, 163
Track in the Fields **54**
Track on the Ice **12**, 30
Trees in Spring **47**, 64
Tribute to Spring **81**, 161
Triple Reflections **63**
Turner, J.M.W. 11, 37
Twins Crater, Vimy Ridge **39**

United Church **92**

Valley, Lake Placid **68**
Van Gogh, Vincent 17, 20, 29
Velásquez, Diego 136
Verandah at Night **66**
Village in the Sun **70**
Village Toward Evening **38**

Water Tank **72**, 114
Waterfall **60**
Waterfront **22**, 39
Waterlilies and the Sunday Paper **96**, 111
Waterlilies in the Cabin **123**, 162
Waterlily **102**
Weed Iron Mines **43**, 79
White Matrix **28**
White Waterfall **58**, 29, 101, 103
Whitman, Walt 32
Wicker Chair **16**, 43
Wilkin, Karen 21
Window **4**, 11
Winter Comes Softly **109**, 163
Wood Interior **31**
Wood, W.J. 29

Yellow Coat **104**
Yonge Street **116**, 167

Zorach, William 12, 13

INDEX

This book was edited
for Douglas & McIntyre by George Payerle,
designed by Robert Bringhurst
and set into type by The Typeworks, Vancouver.
The colour separations were made by Peter Madliger
and the sheets printed under the direction of
Mike Butterfield and Dick Kouwenhoven
at Hemlock Printers, Vancouver.
The binding is by Hans Strohhacker
at Northwest Book Company.

The types used here
are Trajanus roman & italic (for the text),
Kabel (for the captions) and Centaur (on the title page).
The earliest incarnations of these printing types
were cut and cast in metal in Chicago, Offenbach and Frankfurt
between 1914 and 1939.
They were designed, respectively,
by Warren Chappell, Rudolf Koch and Bruce Rogers,
three contemporaries of the painter
David Milne.